COAL MINER'S GRANDDAUGHTER:

CHILDHOOD MEMORIES

JOAN S. HUST

Edited by Jeanette M. Johnson
Printed by GORHAM PRINTING

ISBN   13
978-0-9824415-8-9

ISBN   10
0-9824415-8-4

I dedicate this book to my husband, Bill.
He gives me space to write
and helps me above the call of duty in every area of my life.
I could fill many books with words of love
and still not have shared but
a small portion of how much he means to me.

CONTENTS

Foreword

It has taken me a long time to actually sit down and write memories of my childhood. It is amazing what fun and delight it has given me. And it has made me realize how He has showered me with His love and taken care of me. People from every walk of life have encouraged me to write a book. Here it is. And I look forward to mining many more memories now that I've begun! This is just a sample of what is to come! I trust you will enjoy reading these childhood memories of days gone by.

Preface

I have wanted to put my childhood memories in writing since 1990 when my mother left me to go to a land that is fairer than day. A place where there is no more suffering and living water flows. Oh, I have missed her so much, but I know she is in a far better place now.

At times I'm asked why my memory is so good. And why did I write the book? Pieces of my early life created my passion for written words and capturing memories into stories. It started small. In the beginning my mother's lists inspired me to copy letters from street signs and buildings when we rode the trolley. She faithfully read aloud an encyclopedia as we traveled from state to state. Dad's work was seasonal, and between jobs we always visited grandparents where after dinner we gathered near the big black wood stove and listened to one story after another, precious family times. Mother gave me a daily journal when I was in fifth grade, and I never stopped writing my daily comings and goings. When one of my teachers challenged me to read many books over the summer to catch up with classmates, I learned the importance of letters on book spines in the library.

When I left home I wrote every day to my mother. At the first of a year I addressed envelopes for the entire year. I always carried those addressed stamped envelopes with me to work in my handbag. I did this for forty plus years. I wanted my mother to have something from me in her mailbox every time she went out to get the mail. I thought I was doing this for her. Not true. I soon realized after she was gone that I really missed writing her. No one but my mother would want to hear from me daily. Writing has always been a comfort to me personally. All the stories I write are true. One story leads to another, and all the memories I have are very real to me. It gives me such joy to share them with you. Last, but certainly not least, I write these stories that this book of memories may inspire you to start writing your true and inspiring stories too!

Acknowledgements

I am blessed beyond words that my brother, Leonard, who has gone home to be with the Lord, was such a joy to me as we remembered our fun times together. He and I learned about a family secret when we were adults and married with children of our own. After that we loved each other even more, and we had many two to three hour conversations on the phone weekly. Aunt Catherine as I knew her, Leonard and I had the same voice. Many times people said to us that they didn't know which one of the three of us was on the phone. Leonard truly encouraged me to write my childhood memories.

I am blessed with so many friends that it would be impossible to name them all. They helped me realize how precious memories are. They and my three children, Segred, Pepper, and Jacob, have encouraged me to write. You would never have had the opportunity to read my book if it were not for my outstanding editor, Jeanette Johnson, who encouraged me beyond the gates of glory. Above all, I want to thank Jesus for how my life has changed since I accepted Him as my personal Savior when I was a sophomore in high school.

Trust in the Lord with all your heart,
and lean not on your own understanding.
In all thy ways acknowledge Him,
and He shall direct thy paths.
Proverbs 3:5-6

Introduction

William Robert Dean and Sigrid Virginia Lundgren adopted me when I was young. They loved me very much. I am blessed to have had such caring, thoughtful and wonderful parents. We were a family of three. Life with my parents was unbelievably rich, loving and exciting. We traveled all over the states as my dad was a chef, and we went where he was able to get a job. We loved the West, East Coast, and usually lived in Florida during the tourist season. We lived mostly in Ohio, Michigan and Florida. I was in twenty-five grammar schools before fifth grade and enjoyed all the schools, teachers and classmates.

My story began when I was rescued from a shack in Cleveland, Ohio, where I lived with my biological mother and my brother, Leonard. Uncle Bob, the brother of her dad, Watt, and Sigrid, his girlfriend at the time, rescued us. We had nothing, so Uncle Bob's paycheck bought us clothes, shoes and toys. Helmer came from Byrnedale, Pennsylvania to visit his sister, Sigrid. Helmer fell in love with my biological mother, Catherine Lowena Dean. Catherine and Helmer married, and then she became my Aunt Catherine, and Aunt Sigrid's brother, Helmer became my Uncle Helmer. Leonard stayed with them, and I went with Uncle Bob and Aunt Sigrid. They became my parents, Mom and Dad.

All six of us lived in my dad's one-room apartment on the fourteen floor while Uncle Helmer looked for a job. Leonard and I loved living in the apartment building because we could run up and down the stairs and play on the rooftop, which we called Tar City. Unfortunately for us kids, it only lasted about a month. Uncle Helmer got a job and they moved. My dad wanted to go to Florida to introduce my mom and I to his sister down there. So we drove to Florida and Dad looked for work. I always missed my brother Leonard.

Because my mom wanted to be known as an American, she changed her name from Sigrid to Virginia. Then all of a sudden she changed my name! Everyone was calling me Joanie when my name was Rosemarie. I didn't understand it, but no one talked about it my whole life. Until I was married and had children of my own, I didn't know Aunt Catherine was my biological mother. I went to the memorial service of my father who raised me and there I learned that I was the first-born child of my Aunt Catherine. She was the niece of my father. All those years I'd wondered, Why Are You Calling Me Joanie When My Name Is Rosemarie?

My Big Lollipop

Dad and Leonard

Sledding with Dad

CHAPTER 1

GENTLY NURTURED

The Black Suitcase

"Where is my black suitcase, Mom? I can't find it."

"It's on the top shelf under the two other brown suitcases in the storeroom in the basement. Take the key with you to open the lock, and be careful. What do you want it for?"

"I thought we could play Old Maid this morning with Annie's mom who lives on the 8th floor."

"How do you know if she wants to play cards this morning? This is her washday she signed up for last week. I saw her name on the list in the basement."

"She said she would after the wash is finished, and Annie and I are going to help her hang the clothes on the line. The janitor put up a new line, and made it not so high so Annie and I could reach it and help our mothers."

"Well Joanie. You have done it again. You organized a fun time even though this is a busy washday. I would have never thought of it today. I'll help you get the black suitcase down after I finish Dad's chef shirt."

"Thanks, Mom."

Off I went, skipping and jumping down the fourteen flights of stairs to the basement. Just as I landed on the floor to the basement, I realized I forgot to get the key off the hook in the hall closet, so I had to run back up the fourteen flights of stairs to get it.

"Joanie, you were too fast. I called you, but you didn't hear me. Come over and have a glass of milk and a scone that I just baked with raisins."

"OK, Mom. Thanks. You are the best mom in the world."

I scarfed down the scone in a hurry while slurping my glass of milk to wash it down. Mom's scones were always delicious. Then I went down to the basement again, and this time I didn't hurry so much. I carried the key on a string wrapped around my wrist. It was fun to go in the basement, to walk around and see all the stuff families put in their spaces. Brown and black suitcases sat in practically everyone's space. I always wondered why suitcases didn't come in all colors.

I finally found our space and opened it up. I stood still for a moment and looked at all our stuff. I wondered how it would fit in our car when we hit the road again. The season was almost over, and dad would be out of a job again. Just then I saw the black suitcase and heard my mom's footsteps as she came up behind me. We grabbed the black suitcase and opened it. Sure enough, the set of Old Maid cards was tucked in the corner looking up at us. Mom placed a little rag rug on the floor. We sat down and looked at all the games in my black suitcase.

"Mom, will there be room for my black suitcase in the car when we move?"

"Oh yes, don't worry, Joanie. It's the first item that Dad packs in the trunk." Mom hugged me, and we laughed and hugged each other as we discovered old games that we had forgotten about in the black suitcase.

Trolley Is More Than Just a Ride

My mother made everything a game. I used to watch her write a list to go to the grocery store. Then when she came home she would write beside each item how much it cost. I kept saying I wanted to write a list too. This was before I started kindergarten. Mother suggested I write down every morning what I wanted to do that day. So I would make my one-word list every day and check it off every night after supper. She said that it was like having a diary. The next time my mother went to the store, she brought home a notebook that was black and white, and the pages were sewn with white thread. I was excited to have my own notebook to write in. I carried that notebook everywhere I went.

We used to jump the trolley or bus and go into the city. Can you get an education by riding on a trolley to get around in big cities as a young girl? You bet you can. It was so much fun to hear the accents of people when they jumped on the trolley. After a while you recognized the same folks and it was fun to talk with them. Mother said the usual, "Hello. How are you? Have a good day." When it got crowded, I gave up my seat to an older person and ran up and down from the front to the back, talking, laughing, and playing tag with the kids.

Sometimes the conductor let me stand by him and count the change to give back to persons who didn't have exact change to drop in the money box. If it was the correct amount, you pushed the level for it to drop down inside at the bottom so you didn't see it anymore and the next person to drop the change in the box would not short change you. Sometimes the people denied they didn't put in enough money and the conversation would get hot and heavy. Some told the truth, some didn't, and the conductor told some to get off. When they this happened, they shouted bad words. This caused the trolley to be late, so people going to work started shouting. I was excited to hear all this chatter, but others on the trolley were on a schedule and didn't want to be late. Once in a while when some energetic, boisterous fellas got off, they ran to the back of the trolley, jerked the cords off the overhead wires, and ran like mad. Of course, the trolley couldn't go forward, so the conductor got off, walked around to the back, pushed the cords up to the wires, and walked back shaking his head. When he got back on the trolley, the people cheered. Off we went to the next stop. It was always exciting to ride on the trolley with my mother.

When we took the trolley, we rode all the way to the end of the line and back. We went through several different neighborhoods, and I wrote down the names of some of the streets. They were foreign words: Italian, German, Polish, French, and the hardest street names of all in the Russian section. I loved it. This was a fun game for both Mom and me. I not only learned to write down the names of the streets, but I also recognized them when they were in the newspaper, on signs, and on labels in the department store. The trolley and bus drivers only charged us one fare, as they were fascinated with what we were doing. When school was out, one driver brought his second-grade son; he would sit with us and write down the names of the streets too.

I filled up one notebook after another, so by the time I was ten years old my mother bought me a real diary. It was a small, pretty, maroon, shiny, leather book with gold trim, a page for every day of the week, the word *DIARY* on the cover, and it had a gold clasp with a lock and key. I wrote in it every day. This was the beginning. Mother encouraged me to write, and I would read to my dad and mother every evening when Dad came home from work. Some things I did not read, and they would just smile.

I started writing letters to myself, telling how I felt about certain things. I would write imaginary thank you notes; they came in handy, as I copied them when I received a gift from my aunts and uncles. Once in a while, I pasted a picture in my diary. I began carrying it everywhere. Then I could write anytime, anywhere I felt like it. My diary was and always has been very comforting to me. It is my special friend.

Writing in a diary is an activity accessible to anyone with a pen or pencil and paper or a book with blank pages. Writing doesn't have to take much time. When you hurt and your feelings have been crushed, these writing tips can help you heal: find a time and place where you won't be disturbed, write for a half an hour without stopping, don't think about grammar or spelling, write only for yourself, and write personal feelings that are important to you. A diary's magic can help you release pain, eliminate confusion, clear your head so you can move forward, expand your innate creativity, and help you see the bigger picture that life has for you. Start a diary today if you haven't done so already. It all started for me when, before I was in kindergarten, my mother guided me to write a one-word list of what I wanted to do every day. I still write in my diary every day. It gives me great comfort, healing, and joy. Try it. I know it will do the same for you.

Toys

Every child has toys. I used to love to go to the homes of my friends. They would bring out their boxes and bags of toys. One friend had a barrel on homemade wheels that she rolled out whenever I went over to play. I kept all my games and some toys, if they would fit, in a suitcase, as it was the best way to carry them when we moved so many times. The suitcase fit on the floor way back in the trunk of our Plymouth two-passenger car.

Because of moving, it was unusual to buy anything that was not a necessity. When we were living in Cleveland my mother bought me a child's table with two chairs, a lovely set of china teacups with saucers and tiny plates decorated with pink roses that were made in Britain. She set them on the tablecloth she had made that matched the set. We never had real tea in the cups, but we did have small homemade Swedish scones, tarts, apple cake, ginger cookies, and fruitcake on the tiny plates. I liked the desserts served in small pieces.

My mother sat down with me and we repeated a prayer together that we made up, thanking God for His many blessings. We ended praying for all the children who didn't have food to eat. Sometimes we even sang a song. Our favorite was "Jesus loves me this I know, for the Bible tells me so. Little ones to Him belong. We are weak, but He is strong. Yes, Jesus loves me. Yes, Jesus loves me. Yes, Jesus loves me. The Bible tells me so."

We took turns pretending to pour tea in our cups. I didn't like not having real tea in the cups, so my mother started pouring water from the teapot into our cups. I liked that a lot better. Pretending was very hard for me. I wanted the real thing. I had my first cup of tea when I was ten years old. Mother didn't think children should drink tea so young, and coffee was a "no- no" till you were an adult. She never did serve me coffee even as an adult. She thought it was a bad habit.

When our tea party was over, I was relieved, as I wanted to go outside and climb up my favorite tree before someone else got my spot. Did I enjoy a tea party? In many ways, yes I did. All my girlfriends were jealous, as they didn't have make-believe tea parties in their homes. In many ways, no I didn't. Sometimes I was anxious to get outside to play. My mother always went all out for our tea party. The dessert she made for each party was different. Each time I decided that it was my favorite dessert, no matter what it was. I look back on those tea parties with my mother as loving and precious times that were just for the two of us.

My One and Only Doll

When I was supposed to be asleep at night, I listened to my mom and dad talk in the other room. The reason I could hear them was that my mother was hard of hearing. My dad was always so kind and patient. He never raised his voice even though he had to repeat many sentences.

This night, the big discussion was that my mom said that I should have a doll. What kind should it be? Where should he shop for it when he got paid on Friday? How to surprise me? They wouldn't have to buy any clothes for the doll, as mom wanted to make the clothes with material left over from dresses she made for me. They finally decided it would be a Shirley Temple doll as I loved Shirley Temple, especially in the movie when she sang about a lollipop. I stayed with my aunt in Dearborn when they went shopping. I didn't like to go shopping, and I was thrilled to stay at my aunt's. We walked down to the playground at the school, and then we went to my uncle's ice cream store for an ice cream cone.

The day finally came when I could open the big package. I didn't know what was inside, and I was so excited. Mom helped me unwrap the colorful box carefully, so the paper could be used again. The next day Mom ironed it and put it in the bottom drawer in my bedroom. Inside the box was a beautiful doll. Every hair on her head was in place. She wore a pretty dress with a collar, short sleeves, four buttons, a belt to tie, short socks, and shoes. I held her a long time. I set her on the sofa while I ate, and I set her on the stuffed chair when I went out to play. When I went to bed, I set her up on the dresser. All my friends on the other floors of the apartment building, along with their mothers, came in to see my new doll. Our apartment was like a train station because so many mothers and their daughters came in to see my new doll. I felt very important having such a pretty doll.

My dad came home one day and surprised my mother with a Singer sewing machine and a bolt of blue checked material. Mother learned how to use the new sewing machine and made shirts for Dad, school dresses and pajamas for me, clothes for my doll, kitchen curtains, and tablecloths with the bolt of blue checked material. Finally she divided the rest up and gave it to her three sisters, Emma, Anna, and Clara.

One day after a couple of months, I stood on a chair in my closet and cleared the shelf off all by myself. My mom had made a quilt for my doll, which I still have, and I placed my doll in a comfortable position where anyone could see her when I opened the closet door. I never played with her even though my mother made lovely dresses and pajamas for her. One of the outfits she made was a nurse's uniform with a nurse's hat. I loved my Shirley Temple doll, but I liked playing outside jumping rope, skating, climbing a tree, marbles, and kick the can much better.

Flour Sacks and Feed Sacks

Big sacks from flour or livestock feed were great sources for fabric. My mother looked for the same pattern design, but we never got the same pattern twice. Some flour sacks were printed with designs that looked like curtain material, so she made curtains and pillowcases from those. The white feed sacks made perfect sheets for our beds. Mother really liked flour sacks because after you washed them, the fabric was very soft and nice for sewing. Mother used this fabric a lot to make underwear and clothes for little babies. Many dresses and boys' shirts could be made from these sacks, and sometimes even underpants.

During this time there was a motto, "Repair, reuse, make do, and don't throw anything away." I don't remember people buying clothes at a store. My mother mended socks and sewed patches on all holes in our clothes. I had many cousins on both sides of my parent's families, and Mom handed my clothes down to my cousins when they no longer fit me and visa versa. My mother even saved cotton thread used to sew the sacks together. She saved it all and used it for many projects. With leftover scraps of material, she sewed clothes for my doll. I never really played with my doll, but I liked the clothes my mother made for her.

My mother loved to sew for me, and I loved to wear the dresses she made. She always made each dress different. My mother made dresses with sleeves and without sleeves, with collars and without collars. She made belts and sashes. I had many dresses made out of colorful flour sacks, and I loved them all. A lot of sewing was done just before school started in the fall. A photographer from the other side of town came over to take pictures of the school classes. The girls were all so proud of their dresses, and not one was made by a pattern, yet we all looked alike. The boys wore their new shirts, but always complained that they itched a lot. I could never figure it out. None of us girls talked about being itchy in our new dresses.

Once a month on a Sunday afternoon many families gathered to eat and play together. I liked seeing all the feed sack aprons and their patterns on all our mothers. Each girlfriend argued that her mother wore the most beautiful apron. I was never convinced that any other mother had an apron as beautiful as my mother's. No one I knew had a camera when I was young. What a treat it would be to have photos of all my friends and their mothers in our flour sack dresses and colorful feed sack aprons!

Curlers

I was rummaging through one of my dresser drawers today and came across a dozen of my mother's metal curlers. I'll never forget these curlers as long as I live. They were only about three inches long and had a wire clip-like attachment on them, so you could wind your hair around them and use the clip to hold the hair tight to the curler. After all the curlers were wrapped tightly in place, you sprinkled water on them from the tap.

Mom faithfully went through this exercise every day, including Sunday, one hour before Dad arrived home from work. Dad always worked seven days a week as a chef in the restaurant. I always knew the time was close to Dad's coming home as Mom first changed into a freshly starched, ironed, colorful cotton housedress, and she put her hair up in curlers. She timed his arrival home very well. Our miniature Toy Manchester dog, Toy, barked, pranced, and scratched on the door when Dad was about a block away. Mom took the last curler out and quickly ran the comb through her hair as he was driving into the garage.

Dad quickly opened the screen door and kissed Mom with the greeting, "How pretty you always look!" Toy still barked and now scratched Dad's trouser leg. Dad leaned over, reached in his pocket, and gave him a bone. Then Mom and Dad came and sat in my bedroom with me on the bed, and we talked over everything that took place in our lives during that day. Dad got up after about fifteen minutes. Mom gathered her metal curlers, and the both of them said to me, "Good Night, Joanie dear. I love you." They walked to their bedroom, and the last thing I heard was Mom setting her metal curlers down on the dresser.

Toothbrush

I first remember brushing my teeth sitting on the wobbly, iron railing holding a mug of water with my toothbrush in it, on the small porch of our fourteenth-floor apartment in the city. I was a child not quite old enough for preschool. It was a challenge for me to straddle the railing while brushing my teeth, looking at the apartment building just a few yards away. I saw a mother at the stove and her children sitting at their table eating breakfast in the kitchen window across from where I was sitting.

It was a nice day. The sun was shining, and their window was open. Her children noticed me, got up, and ran to the window, waved their hands, smiled and giggled at me brushing my teeth. Their mother came to the window and pushed them aside, as she leaned out and screamed at me to get off the railing, or I would fall, hit the sidewalk, and die. My mother, who was in the kitchen preparing our breakfast, heard the screaming and came running out to the porch to see what was the matter. My mother stopped and just looked at me. She seemed very nervous and upset. She was not smiling, but said very gently to come on in, as she had my favorite breakfast ready to eat. Before she could reach me, I jumped down and told her that I brushed every tooth just like she showed me.

As we were eating, she told me that the iron railing was not the place to brush my teeth. It was a bad example for Mrs. Francisco's small children, and it made her blood pressure rise, which was not good for her health, as Mrs. Francisco was going to have her fifth child in a couple of months. I promised my mother that I would not sit on the iron railing anymore to brush my teeth. I liked Mrs. Francisco and her children, and I wanted to be a good girl, so she would not have high blood pressure. I was anxious to see her new baby, as they wanted a girl after having four boys, and I did not want her new baby girl to have a red face like Mrs. Francisco had when she screamed at me.

The next morning when I was walking out to the porch with my mug of water and toothbrush, my mother went with me. She had a three-foot ladder set up with a colorful securely-fastened cushion on the top of the ladder for me to sit on. I loved it. It was set behind the iron railing back near the door. She held my mug of water and toothbrush as I stepped up to the top and sat down. She gave me my mug and my toothbrush. She kissed and hugged me. She said, "Brush every tooth well. Wave to Mrs. Francisco and the children! Now you can see more than just straight ahead. You can see in all directions, north, south, east and west. Have a fun, good tooth-brushing time. I'll call you when breakfast is ready."

Two Weekly Errands

My mother had me do two errands every week without exception. They were the butcher shop and the cleaners. Neither one of these was nearby. They involved catching trolleys and getting transfers to other lines. It was all fun to me, and I enjoyed it. Parents of my friends I played with never allowed their children to take this on, but I enjoyed it. It was fun meeting all the people and the drivers on the trolley. They became my extended family. I knew them all by name, and sometimes a driver had a signal where I pretended to pay. I got a Vernors Ginger Ale to drink and brought the driver back a bottle too.

To this day, I love Vernors Ginger Ale. It is America's oldest surviving soft drink. James Vernor, a Detroit pharmacist invented it in 1866. Its slogan, "deliciously different," is really true. The bottling plant and headquarters was a whole city block on Woodward Avenue in Detroit, one block from the Detroit River. My dad, mom and I got together with my mom's sister and family and we all went down for a Vernors Ginger Ale float. Its classic logo was Woody, the gnome mascot.

One day I went to the cleaners, usually on Mondays and got my dad's seven chef shirts for the week. Each one had ten buttons and long sleeves. Each was made of thick, white cotton material, starched. And they were very heavy to carry. The Chinese owner said to me, "No tickee, no laundry." The first time I went after four long bus-rides on a very hot summer day and did not remember to bring the ticket. My mother called to me from the fourteenth floor window, waving the ticket when I was leaving, but I didn't hear her. That only happened once. After that I always had the ticket with me.

Friday was the day to go to the butcher shop. I used to love to go to the butcher shop located off the main street in Detroit near the river. The floor was covered in sawdust. The butcher was a friendly Italian man with plastered-down, black, shiny hair. He spoke broken English and had a smile from ear to ear. He would say, "Ah, Joanie. What does your mother want today? I know she likes lamb or beef roast that she can have for Sunday dinner, and the rest of the week make sandwiches, meatloaf, and soup."

"I want to tell her that you are out of lamb roasts, so I will take the best beef roast that you have today. Now make sure you give me the best one, so I don't have to come back here again. Last week I had to come back here three times."

"I know you did, but your mama did not know, and I don't want you to tell her that I sent the same beef roast back, but I did a little carving to make it look like a different one. You are a good girl not to tell her what I did. Here, sit down, and my wife will make you a good beef sandwich with a whole pickle that you like before you start back home on trolley number seven."

"Thanks a lot. I love to come here but only once a day." This was a good day because my mother liked the roast, I had a good sandwich with a big pickle, and I only had to make one trip to the butcher shop.

Back Door of the Restaurant

I loved to go in the back door of the restaurant where my dad worked. When I walked down the sandy, two-car tracks in the alley, I first came to the back of the restaurant where I saw the outdoor help. Potato and carrot peelers splashed in big buckets of water to wash the vegetables. Rickety old tables held tools for cutting. Garbage cans held all the peelings. The workers drew straws from behind one of their backs, to see who got to take the peelings home. The one who drew the longest straw was the winner, and they smiled and jumped for joy.

These workers in the back hummed and sang songs like my favorite, *Oh! Susanna*. I loved hearing them sing. I also liked *I've Been Working on the Railroad*. They were a happy group of people. I usually sat on one of their laps and jumped down to run and hug my dad when he came out to see if they were getting their work done. Dad lifted me up and hugged and kissed me on the cheek.

After a while I got hungry, even though they'd given me a slice of the raw vegetables they were peeling and cutting up, so I went in the back screen door. I walked around and said "Hello" to everyone and looked at what they were doing. I was fascinated with the baking of pies, cobblers, and cakes, but especially the pie and cobbler dough. They swirled it around and around, then swung it and threw it up in the air, never failing to catch it. Everyone laughed at their techniques. Cherry pies and fruit cobblers were my favorites.

One of the men moved a stool so I could sit up at the long kitchen table. The help took turns getting me something to eat. I liked everything. I always had a small cup of soup, followed by a scoop of mashed potatoes with red gravy. They put ketchup in the gravy to make it red just for me. Quite full by then, I had only a very small piece of fish, my favorite, but I had to save room for dessert. Each time I had a different dessert, so that by the end of the week I'd tasted them all. One of the kitchen help then walked me home. I enjoyed their talk about family, where they were born, and their dreams of owning their own restaurant someday. My mother was always on the lookout for me and met me at the door to thank the help for walking me home.

Lollipop for Joanie

It was Saturday afternoon and the three of us were walking in the city park in Winter Haven, Florida. We were all dressed up. My dad wore a navy blue suit with a white shirt and a blue and red tie. My mother really looked terrific in her streamlined, cream-colored dress, outlined in rusty-brown seams and open-toed brown, shiny shoes. We had only been in Florida five days and were going to meet Uncle Joe and Aunt Helen from Detroit. I was told they were not really my aunt and uncle, but we felt part of the family, as Uncle Joe was my mother's sister's brother-in-law.

My daddy and mommy walked over with their hands behind their backs. "Guess who has something for you," said Mommy, "and it is the biggest you can buy."

"It is red and has a stick on it," said Daddy.

"I don't think I know anything that has a stick on it. Oh, maybe I do. Is it a sailboat like the ones you see in the water at the beaches where we go to build sand castles here in Florida?"

"Now you have to be a little careful, as you have your pretty, new, orchid dress on that has silver bells as buttons, and you don't want to get it all sticky and messy, " said Mommy.

"Oh, I'll be careful. Just tell me what it is!" I said.

"Oh, we can't do that till you take at least another guess," said Daddy.

"Well, it's not a sailboat. Maybe it's something to go with my tea set." All three of us started laughing, and I was jumping up and down. Daddy and Mommy moved slowly around me, and I was getting so excited. Then all of a sudden Mommy and Daddy both held on to the stick, and at the other end was the biggest red lollipop in the whole wide world, and it was all for me.

"Oh, how I love my lollipop! It is the biggest lollipop in the whole wide world! Thank you, Daddy and Mommy! This is fun! I never knew that I would ever have such a big lollipop all to myself!"

Mother reminded me how she made my dress just like the Shirley Temple dress in the big department store window we saw when we were shopping. When we went to a third grade school play, we heard a school class singing *On the Good Ship Lollipop*. The three of us sang this song every night when Daddy came home from work. It was so much fun. The three of us knew all the words by heart. My folks started singing, and I tore the see-through paper off and started licking away.

ON THE GOOD SHIP LOLLIPOP

Shirley Temple 1934

I've thrown away my toys
Even my drum and train.
I wanna make some noise
With real live aeroplanes.

Some day I'm going to fly
I'll be a pilot too.
And when I do, how would you
Like to be my crew?
On the good ship lollipop
It's a sweet trip to a candy shop.
Where bonbons play
On the sunny beach of Peppermint Bay.

Lemonade stands everywhere
Crackerjack bands fill the air.
And there you are!
Happy landing on a chocolate bar.

See the sugar bowl do the tootsie roll
With the big bad devils food cake
If you eat too much ooh ooh
You'll awake with a tummy ache.

On the good ship lollipop
It's a night trip into bed you hop.
And dream away
On the good ship lollipop.

I licked and licked as much as I could, while everyone was talking and laughing. I licked till I could not lick anymore. Whew! I was exhausted. The sun was shining, and I was sticky and hot. All of a sudden I felt sleepy. The next thing I knew, my mommy was saying, "Lollipop girl, upsey daisy." It was time to go to dinner with Uncle Joe and Aunt Helen.

I had been asleep for at least an hour or so, and I felt so good. My poor lollipop melted on my dress, socks, shoes and the bench where I was sitting and had fallen asleep. Everyone was in such a good mood that it didn't matter that I'd made a royal mess of my beautiful, new dress Mother had made.

We all went to a restaurant in Uncle Joe's black Cadillac, which was very nice and roomy. Daddy sat in the front seat with Uncle Joe, and Aunt Helen sat in the back with Mommy and me. Now five people were singing the lollipop song and laughing! When we got to the restaurant Mommy took me to the "little girl's room", as she called it, and washed me from head to toe. The lollipop was even in my hair.

We went out to the table to join the others. When it was my turn to order, the waitress said, "If you eat all your dinner, I have a special lollipop just for you."

"Oh, no thank you. I don't think I want dessert tonight."

Then someone put a nickel in the jukebox. Guess what Shirley Temple was singing. None other than *On the Good Ship Lollipop*! Dad started singing along, and everyone in the restaurant began singing with him. Then one after another, a person would go up and put their nickel in the slot, and my lollipop song played over and over again. Dinner was over and they were still singing as we walked back to the car.

The first thing my neighborhood friend said to me in the morning when I went out to play, "Hey, Joanie! Let's go to the store today and buy a big lollipop."

"Ummm. I don't think so."

Out the Window It Goes

I specifically remember one of many fun trips with my mom, uncle, and aunt for a very special reason.

"Hurry up, Joanie! Uncle Ed and Aunt Emma just got here and beeped that funny-sounding horn on their new black Buick!"

"I'm almost ready. I just had to take my shoes off again, as I forgot to put my socks on first. I don't like these brown high top shoes. I like my play, high top shoes better."

"Why, Joanie? Daddy just bought you these when he got paid yesterday. They are lovely and shiny, plus the laces look so clean, not like the laces in your old shoes."

"Ahhh! I have them on, so I'm ready to go. I'll race you down the flights of stairs!"

"Be careful! You always win. I don't go too fast, as I don't want to slip and fall, and I don't want you to slip and fall either like you do once in awhile when you are in a hurry, and both of your knees have scabs to prove it!"

"Ok, Mom. I'll be careful. We can sit in the back seat and each of us have a window."

Uncle Ed and Aunt Emma were outside waiting for us. We hugged and kissed and clamored into the car. We laughed and talked. All of a sudden, when we were bumper to bumper, the engine got too hot. Uncle Ed stopped, got out of the car, and put the hood up. The radiator was steaming. Very carefully and slowly Uncle Ed wound the cap of the radiator, and before you could say, "Jack Rabbit," the cap went flying! You would have thought it was the Belle Isle Fountain spurting high up into the hood. Other cars had the same problem. All the men had their good shirts off. They had on only their white, 3-strap undershirts.

I got out of the car and started running in and out between all the cars, as Aunt Emma and my mom tried to keep up with me. I was having a fun time and was very excited, but they didn't share my enthusiasm. Uncle Ed finally poured water into the radiator, and we drove over the MacArthur Bridge onto Belle Isle. I loved going to Belle Isle Park, as it was the largest city island park. My dad told me it was larger than Central Park in New York City, which we often went to when we lived in New York City. Each time we went to Belle Isle Park, we took turns visiting the conservatory, botanical gardens, aquarium, museum, marble lighthouse, or canoe ride. I loved walking, skipping, running, and climbing trees along the Detroit River. We had hot dogs and lemonade from home to eat and drink. We sat where we could view downtown Detroit. I woofed down my food and drink in a hurry so that I could join the kids in the water at the fountain. That felt so good. I forgot to take off my shoes and socks, so I went barefoot the rest of the day. Later in the car, one of my wet shoes was in my way, so I threw it out the window during another traffic jam. Oh, oh, what will Daddy say?

My Favorite Place

What a wonderful, fun life I experienced, traveling to so many cities and states with my dad and mom. We were in a different city and state three to five times a year, if not more. While Dad drove us to the next place, my mother read to us for many hours from a one-volume encyclopedia. Sometimes I got to sit in Dad's lap and help him drive. Mom read every section, except math and science. When she finished the encyclopedia, she started over again. Dad and I loved Mom reading to us. Mom could read well because she had completed six years in a one-room schoolhouse and won all the spelling bees and reading competitions. She read her dad's books in Swedish at home. The windy and sometimes single lane roads were not as well maintained as the highways and freeways are today, so it took a long time to go from the South to the North.

We moved many times because my dad had to go where there was work. He could barely read and write his name. I had the honor of teaching him how to read and write. Every evening when he came home from work, I explained everything I had learned at school. He must have been interested, as his job was a 12-hour-seven-days-a-week position as a chef. I watched him kiss Mom every morning, and he had a skip to his walk. When he returned home in the evening, he was slow and dragged his feet a little when he walked up the steps to the house. It was always exciting to see him, as he kissed us both. I sat in his lap and went over all my lessons.

I feel blessed that I saw so much of the United States growing up. Our cars were mostly coupes, so that meant the three of us sat in the front seat. My mom always sat in the middle, as I got carsick easily and had to hang my head out the window many a time.

We were usually in the South during the winter. We always wanted to see something new, so we went to a different city every time we went to Florida, Texas, Arizona, Kentucky, Pennsylvania, and California. Dad always asked us where we wanted to go after each season ended, and we chose the city. I learned to swim at an early age, and I liked the coasts of Florida, especially the Gulf of Mexico. I enjoyed all the sightseeing in all of the states, but I loved jumping the waves in the Gulf of Mexico.

When we went north, Mom and I loved the big cities. My dad told us after a couple of days on the road to make up our mind where we wanted to go, as he would have to turn off this road soon. We varied between Detroit, Cleveland, Lexington, Philadelphia, Phoenix, Santa Barbara, and on and on it went. I had souvenirs from every place we lived for a short time. The souvenirs said "Made in Japan" - today they say "Made in China".

Everywhere we lived my dad enrolled me in school the day we arrived, after we rented an apartment. Every Sunday my mom took me to a church in the neighborhood. She stood outside the church and told me to ask the man at the door where Sunday school class was held. When it was over my mom was outside waiting for me. She took me every Sunday in rain, sunshine, or snow.

I made many friends in my new school, in the Sunday school class, with the kitchen staff at the restaurant and at music and tap dance lessons. I also made friends when we stopped at plantations in the South during the eleven-to-one lunchtime. It was fun watching and talking to the kids my age picking cotton. They gave me some cotton to take back to my classes in the North. They touched my red hair and then looked at their hands. "Get your cotton-pickin' hands off me!" is a phrase holding meaning in the South because their hands were scratchy from the work they did in the fields. How could I describe this to my classes in the North? I heard the workers singing in the fields and swinging and swaying while they sang "All day, all night, angels watchin' over me, my Lord." How could I describe that to my classes in the North?

When we traveled in the summer, it would get very hot, and we felt very sticky. My dad bought a coolator for the car window that he poured water into. It was very noisy, but it kept us much more comfortable when traveling. During WWII, we had to stop for inspection and questioning when we crossed the border to another state. One time as we were going to enter California, the officer told us that we couldn't take our fruit and eggs that we had in our basket. My folks were upset, but my dad solved the problem. He fried the eggs on the fender of our car, and we ate some of the fruit. What we did not eat, he gave to the children hanging around us.

It is not difficult to tell which place I really loved the most. I liked every city and state. I liked all the new friends in school, every schoolteacher, all the kids in the Sunday school classes, my dance and music teachers, and the kitchen staff at all the hotels and restaurants, the plantation cooks, and the kids that picked cotton. Yet my favorite place was not any of those. Even though I really loved them all, had a lot of fun, and everyone gave me a lot of attention, my favorite place was on my daddy's lap.

Red Snowsuit

"Hurry up, Joanie! We have to leave. Dad has a job in Winter Haven."

"Ok. Where is Winter Haven?"

"Winter Haven is in the middle of Florida."

"What are you looking for?"

"My red snowsuit. I can't find it. Where is it?"

"You don't need to take it. We are going to sunny Florida where the sun shines all the time. You are going to love it. Just think, no more cold gray-sky days."

"I don't like sunny weather. It makes me feel hot and my skin icky and wet. Why do we have to go? I like it here."

"Oh, Joanie. You are going to have such a good time. We're going to live where there are more orange trees than you can count. You can pick as many oranges as you want to, and we can squeeze, squeeze, squeeze all the oranges from early morning to late at night. We'll drink until we float and our skin turns orange. Orange juice is your very favorite drink, and this won't come from a can or the frozen section at the grocery store. It will be fresh and delicious. We're going to have so much fun."

I started to cry and sob. My mother picked me up, and I saw my red snowsuit in one of the boxes. I grabbed it, as my dad took me in his arms and carried me out to the car. He put me in the middle of the front seat, tenderly spreading my red snowsuit under me, so I could sit on it. My mother was seated beside me and flipped the pages open to read from her one-volume wine-colored encyclopedia she always kept in the car. Dad and I really loved to hear Mother read to us while he drove. I finally stopped crying, settled down, nestled close to my dad, and Mother began reading from the literature section. Before I knew it, I was hearing my dad singing softly in my ear, trying gently to wake me up for lunch at a red, white and blue metal-looking diner beside the highway. I scrambled out of the car and raced to be the first one to open the screen door. The jukebox was blaring the song *Alexander's Ragtime Band*. I still wanted to turn around and go back home. Dad said we wouldn't stay too long, he had a job to go to, so it was best we go to Winter Haven, Florida. He said I would feel much better after I ate my meat loaf and mashed potatoes. I did feel a lot better after I ate, but I still wanted to go back home. When a car passed on the narrow windy road, one of the cars had to get half off the road, so the cars wouldn't hit each other. It took four long days of driving and three nights of sleeping over in people's homes to get there. When we got to a town, we drove up and down the streets looking for a sign on the lawn of a home that said "One-night Room for Rent with Breakfast $2.00".

We left early in the morning after breakfast, as the weather was getting warmer, which I did not like at all. Our two-door, one-seat, black Plymouth coupe seemed to shrink in size when the weather was hot. When it got that hot, our clammy arms stuck to each other even with the two windows rolled all the way down to let in breezes.

"Mom, tell me what Winter Haven looks like, and why do we have to go there? Can't Dad get a job where it's cool weather?"

Even though I was talking to my mom, Dad spoke up right away, "I can get a job up North, but mother has sinus problems and she is very uncomfortable in the cold winters. I think it will be good for her and all of us to enjoy warmer weather, swim in the Gulf of Mexico an hour or so away, and be in a place where the sun is shining every day."

"Here is what I read about Winter Haven, Joanie. It is called "The Chain of Lakes City" because it has so many fresh water lakes right in the city. The lakes are connected by canals they call "Chain of Lakes." Major league baseball teams come there for their spring training. Cypress Gardens is a big theme park. They are known for their orange groves as far as your eyes can see. I am happy for their lowest temperature of 62 degrees which will be good for me."

"How hot is that, Mother?"

"You might think it's hot at first, but it really isn't."

When we finally got to Winter Haven there was a big park in the center of town. My dad got out of the car and walked over to an older couple sitting on a green wooden bench. He asked if they knew where Mr. and Mrs. Westfall lived. "Sure do," said the man. "Everyone knows the Westfall's. They have the most acreage of all who have orange groves." He stood up, gave my dad directions and said he could not miss their house that had a porch the length of the house. "They are fine people, and hire many local people to work for them."

Dad thanked him and tipped his hat as he climbed back in the car and drove away.

It seemed like just a few minutes and we drove into their driveway. Mr. and Mrs. Westfall came out to greet us with their daughter, Betty. They walked us down the path to a very nice guesthouse that they fixed up for us to live in, so dad could go to work in the morning. Dad was a chef at the military base close by, and we saw many young men in uniform walking up and down the narrow road to town.

One day I told my mother that I was going to walk back up North, as each day got hotter and hotter. I put on my wool, red snowsuit and hollered, "Goodbye! " as I waved to my mother. It was a long walk through the orange grove, but I finally came to the highway. By this time I was really hot. My snowsuit was wet, and I felt a little dizzy and hungry too. Before leaving, I had pulled off a couple of oranges and jammed them in my pockets.

The next thing I knew I was at the front door of our house, and a policeman had me in his arms. He was talking to my mother. My mother had tears in her eyes and was frightened when she opened the door and saw the policeman holding me in his arms.

"Joanie! Joanie! Are you sick? Where have you been? I have been calling for you for the last hour."

The policeman said he had a call from the rancher down the road that a little girl in a red snowsuit was laying on the road. He went to the rescue right away and picked her up. He gave her water from his tin cup he always had with him. The little girl told him her name and where she lived. She said she didn't mean to be bad, but she wanted to walk back North where the weather was cooler.

My mother thanked the policeman for bringing me home, and she carried me to the little cot under the dining room window where there always seemed to be a little breeze.

"I'm sorry, Mother. I just wanted to go back home. "

"When we go back home after WWII, we'll all go together. Right now, just rest till Dad comes home. You have quite a story to tell him, Joanie."

"Mother, will you keep my snowsuit close by me?"

"I'll spread it out on the back of the chair by your bed. The red matches the color of the roses outside your window."

"Thanks, Mother."

"You're welcome, Joanie dear."

Sledding

Most of my youth till about junior high school, I lived in one of the big cities in the eastern United States in an apartment building with fourteen floors or more. Of course, the best floor was the rooftop we called Tar City.

In the winter, all of us kids built forts between the apartment buildings and had snowball ball fights. We built snowmen on the roof of the building and went to nearby parks to go sledding. One of the parks I liked the most had hills we sled on and ponds that were frozen over for ice skating. I loved sledding, but I was not very good at ice skating, as my feet got too cold and I had weak ankles. My mother took me to her sister's house when all the neighbors got together and flooded their backyards so we could skate. One of the games that was so much fun, but scary for me, was when a dozen kids held onto a rope and were pulled very fast. The only way we could let go and be free was to grab on to a tree and drop the rope.

I loved sledding outside, going up and down the hill lying on my dad's back. My dad was longer than the sled, and I held onto his shoulders. He called out, "Ready, Joanie?" And down we went, sliding on the icy hill. Our sled was made of several slats of wood with steel runners and red handles for steering. It was exciting whooshing down the hill trails with the cold wind in my face as the sled went from left to right, and up and down the sides of the trail. My dad made sure the runners were sharpened to cut through the ice that builds up in the trails. My mother was scared to go down the hill on a sled, so she watched us. I heard her scream once when we missed what we called the speed bump and we went into a big drift of snow. Within minutes people were helping us get out. I never lost my grip on my dad's shoulders.

My dad and I never stopped sledding till our faces and hands and feet had nearly turned to ice. Our faces were bright red and cold. We got in the car and took our boots and scarves off. Mom had dry socks and another one of her knitted scarves ready for us. On the way home, we always stopped by one of mom's brother's or sister's houses to tell about our sledding. Of course, we all laughed a lot as we greatly embellished the tales of our adventures.

Spitz Billy

The summer before I started school, my dad got a job as a chef in the small resort town of Willoughby, Ohio, a suburb of Cleveland where I was born. We lived on the outskirts of town in a rented house that was furnished with a wood stove for cooking, a wraparound porch, an acre of land, and best of all Billy, a white, thick-furred, fluffy, curly-tailed Spitz dog who followed me everywhere from the time I woke up in the morning until I fell asleep at night with him next to my bed under the open window.

Billy was a beautiful, loving, bright and fun dog. The neighbors liked him because he went hunting with their husbands and liked their children. To me, he looked like the American Eskimo dog.

My dad found a small red wagon and a dog harness in the barn one day. The harness fit Billy, so Dad attached it to the red wagon that was in the barn beside a huge pile of hay. I climbed in the wagon and sat down. I said,

"Giddyup, Billy!" And he pulled me up and down the dirt road every day. At first my mother walked beside us, but after a few days she let us go alone.

One day the three of us walked down to the river. Billy stopped and sat down under the tree in the shade. Mother and I walked in the shallow, cool, ripply water. It felt so refreshing that we thought Billy should cool off too. We unhooked him from the wagon and coaxed him to come in the water, but he was hesitant. So I started splashing him and smoothing his white, furry hair. He let me play with him, and then he shook himself. It was so funny to watch. Eventually I held onto his harness, and we walked in the water together. Because the water was so shallow, I could sit down and put my hands together and pour water on Billy's face and then smooth his thick fur. He didn't budge, so he must have liked it.

We thought we were only going to live in Willoughby for the summer, but they asked my dad to stay on through the winter. Mom and I were excited because we enjoyed the area. Every day Mom and I went for walks with Billy. My folks bought a small sled, and Billy pulled me on my sled, and my mother walked beside me. When we came back home after the long walk, we played in the snow. Then the three of us stood around the wood stove, while I pulled icicles off Billy's fur. He stood still and licked my hand. It was a harsh, snowy, windy winter, but Mother bundled me up to go out. Every day was a new adventure of fun for the three of us. My mother was a good sport and very creative. When my dad came home after the dinner meal at the end of the day, we all sat around the wood stove with Billy next to me and talked about our day until we were ready to hit the city of bedsprings.

Lundgren's Ice Cream Store

It was always exciting when tourist season was over in the South. Dad packed up his knives, meat and fishhooks, thermometers, meat mallet, sharpening steel, meat hammer, and his meat cleavers. I would help him sometimes, as I could tell his tools. They had an X carved on each one. He took a very close look at all the tools in the kitchen, and he had a numbered list that mom wrote out of the name of each tool he owned. Dad was always well liked by the kitchen staff everywhere he worked and there was never a tool missing. After he collected them all, I read the list as he placed them in his wood toolbox. Mom was packed up when Dad came home, and the plan was always to get a good night's sleep and leave early in the morning. That always worked out well.

Dad and mom packed up the black Dodge and we left by the crack of dawn. I read the road signs and we always headed north. The first question Dad asked Mom and me was always, "Where do we want to go and live for the next three or four months? Joanie needs to enroll in school right away." Mom and I would suggest Chicago, Cleveland where I was born, Lexington near Dad's sisters, or Dearborn where Mom's sister and two brothers lived. This time, it so happened that the three of us wanted to go to Dearborn, especially me as I loved to go to my uncle's ice cream store. He always gave me the latest flavor of ice cream in a nice cone that he made. It was a three-day two-night drive to get there, which seemed forever. All I could think about was Lundgren's Ice Cream Store and all the flavors of ice cream.

When we arrived late one afternoon, we went directly to my aunt's house. I ran in the side door and down the steps and there was my aunt taking clothes out of the wringer washing machine. She hugged me and we climbed back up the stairs just as my mom and dad got out of the car. She had our beds made up. I always slept upstairs with my cousins, and Mom and Dad had the guest bedroom downstairs. Mom helped my aunt prepare dinner and set the table. It was so fun to see my uncle when he drove up and parked beside the curb at the front of the house.

After dinner, Uncle said there would be a special dessert. I guessed and guessed what it would be, but never guessed the right answer. Then he said, "Let's all walk down to Ford Road by way of Kendal." He always teased me and said that we didn't need to have dessert tonight. It was a nice time of evening to walk with my two cousins, Mom and Dad, and my aunt and uncle. My cousins knew where we were going, but I didn't know it was the way to get to my uncle's ice cream store. When I saw it, I was really excited and could hardly wait to go through the door. My uncle pretended the door wouldn't open. A two-scoop ice cream cone with the flavor of my choice was the perfect way to end a perfect day.

Now I Lay Me Down To Sleep

Every night of my life in my parents' home, my mother and I said this prayer in unison:

Now I lay me down to sleep,
I pray the Lord my soul to keep;
If I die before I wake,
I pray the Lord my soul to take.

It was always a precious time. My mother tucked me in and sort of fussed over me by gently rubbing my cheeks and touching my nose, making sure I was comfortable, kissing me good night, and saying, " I love you, Joanie dear," and I would say, "I love you too, Mommy." I have heard other versions of this prayer throughout the years, but this one will always hold a special place in my heart.

I was friendly as a child, and I would have one or two girlfriends stay over for a slumber party. They weren't familiar with this prayer, so my mother taught them, and they not only said it at bedtime, but also all day everywhere we went the following day. Two weeks later my mother took us to the park that had the highest slide. When we climbed up all the steps to the top, it was rather scary the first time. One of my friends blurted this prayer out loud and clear before she sat and slid down the slide. After that, we all said the prayer before we went down that slide.

Even though this prayer was written to say before going to sleep at night, the teacher in our school class liked it and taught it to her students at Southside Elementary.

This prayer has always been a part of my life. I have used it in many years of teaching in the USA and in Third World countries overseas. It has been translated into several languages. It is a classic children's prayer from the 18th century. This version is in The New England Primer.

Joan and Grandma Lundgren

Hilma and Arvid Lundgren

Aunt Catherine and Mom and Me (Leonard)

Mom and Dad and Me (Leonard)

CHAPTER 2

UNCONDITIONALLY LOVED

8 Leg Turkey

Have you ever seen a turkey with eight legs? Well, at Thanksgiving dinner at my grandparents' house, their turkey had eight legs! Eight of us grandchildren sat on the benches at their Thanksgiving dinner table. Grandpa, who sat at the head of the table, always served everyone the main dish. Grandma sat at the other end and Grandpa said the blessing. It was always long because there were so many of us, and he mentioned everyone in his prayer. When he finished, he stood, and Grandma passed our plates to him. He cut and served the meat. He asked what piece of meat you preferred, and our folks answered: "light," "dark," or "it didn't matter." All of us grandchildren said, "The leg." Grandpa and Grandma just smiled. I just hoped and held my breath that one of the two legs would be mine. I only wanted a leg because all of us wanted one, and we all knew there were only two. I actually liked the white meat the best.

I never understood why we had to wait till everyone was served before we could eat, but that was the way it was. And none of us started before the other. When all the adults had been served, they seemed content to smile and wink at each other. Here I was jittery as a jitterbug waiting for Grandpa to serve the rest of us. Grandma then told us that the mashed potatoes were not quite ready yet. My cousin next to me whispered in my ear that he didn't care about the mashed potatoes; all he cared about was the leg of the turkey.

I thought the same way, but we didn't say anything. Grandma passed the rest of the plates up to Grandpa. He put four plates on one side of him, and four plates on the other side of him. He took his time and smiled at us with a twinkle in his eye. Then he talked to us about fairness and how in life we had to accept everything that came our way. Then he went on and on about how we would not always be the winner. Someone had to lose. He said that there can be joy in losing even though we don't feel joy at first when we lose, but that down the road when we look back, everything that happens to us works out for the best. My cousins on each side of me kept nudging me under the table. I was trying to keep a straight face and not budge, but I really wanted to get back at them with a twisted pinch that would make them cry out for mercy. But no, I was a good girl, so my parents would be proud of me. It got to be ridiculous, as everyone kept looking and smiling at the eight of us. They even winked at us. I began to wonder where those two legs of the turkey were. I thought by this time that there weren't any legs at all! Maybe they had been badly bruised, and Grandpa didn't have the two legs. Now Grandpa looked at our four plates on each side of him. He counted them to make sure he had enough plates. I was wondering what he would put on the six plates that were left after he put a leg on two of the plates.

To make the whole situation worse, one of my uncles started singing this hymn. *Come Ye Thankful People, Come.* Everyone joined him, including Grandpa.

COME, YE THANKFUL PEOPLE, COME

Come, ye thankful people, come, raise the song of harvest home;
All is safely gathered in, ere the winter storms begin.
God our Maker doth provide for our wants to be supplied;
Come to God's own temple, come, raise the song of harvest home.
All the world is God's own field, fruit unto His praise to yield;
Wheat and tares together sown unto joy or sorrow grown.
First the blade and then the ear, then the full corn shall appear;
Lord of harvest, grant that we wholesome grain and pure may be.

For the Lord our God shall come, and shall take His harvest home;
From His field shall in that day all offenses purge away,
Giving angels charge at last in the fire the tares to cast;
But the fruitful ears to store in His garner evermore.
Even so, Lord, quickly come, bring Thy final harvest home;
Gather Thou Thy people in, free from sorrow, free from sin,
There, forever purified, in Thy garner to abide;
Come, with all Thine angels come, raise the glorious harvest home.

Grandpa now made the announcement that we should put our heads down on the table, close our eyes, and leave enough room for our plate to be set down. When he said, *"Leg Time!"* everyone could open his or her eyes. We all looked at each other, but did as we were told. We could hear the plate being set down in front of us. I was dying to open my eyes, but I waited patiently to hear Grandpa say *"Leg Time."* He finally said the words, *"Leg Time,"* and it was music to my ears.

Guess what? All eight of us had a turkey leg on our plate! Everyone clapped their hands, and laughed uncontrollably. Oh, what a fun experience! I'll never forget Grandpa and Grandma's eight-leg turkey.

Just to let you know how it happened that there were eight legs. The neighbors had given them to my grandparents, as this was a very special occasion, having eight grandchildren for Thanksgiving dinner.

Childhood Christmas

Many memories come to my mind as I think about Christmas as a child. The first Christmas Eve I remember is back at my grandma's house in Pennsylvania. My grandpa worked in the coal mines, so that makes me a coal miner's granddaughter.

Christmas Eve we lay on our backs under the branches of the Christmas tree and ate candy popcorn balls that hung from the tree. There were several of us, and I always chose the popcorn ball hanging closest to the floor. They were ever so sweet and tasty. The tree was so pretty with lit wax candles made during summer. We all went to both the Swedish and English services at church.

My grandpa always stood at the door pounding his foot on the floor to get everyone to hurry, as being late was frowned upon. It was fun to sing all the Christmas hymns in both Swedish and English. Grandpa read the Bible in Swedish, and Uncle Emel read it in English. When the offering was taken, Grandpa stood beside each row, and if he was not satisfied with what was in the basket at the end of the pole, he passed it back down the row again. Us kids always thought the sermon was too long, but when the pastor finished and everyone said, "AMEN!" we rushed up to the altar and stood in line, as each one of us received an orange, apple, criss cross red and white candy, and a slab of peanut brittle. A hot cinnamon-smelling drink was served to the older folks. This particular Christmas, Aunt Minnie's dad gave all of us kids a ride up and down the snow-packed road. He was Native American and spoke very little English and operated the livery stable in town. We sang carols till our throats were hoarse and dry.

Christmas morning when we woke up, we smelled cardamom rolls, bread, and coffee. My mother and aunts were all in the kitchen fixing something for the big smorgasbord in the afternoon. The men were bringing in buckets of water from the well, and coal and logs for the kitchen stove. The cast iron potbelly stove in the living room heated the whole house. It heated so well that even though the snow was over our heads, we had to open the windows upstairs, as it got so hot. Older cousins brought in cakes, meat, and potatoes from the dirt cellar under the house. My cousins and I were stringing hot taffy candy on piles of clean snow. Then we built forts, threw snowballs at each other till we were thoroughly exhausted, and called a truce. Everyone came out of their forts, lay down on the ground, and made angels in the snow. You had to be very careful when you got up, as if you stepped on a snow angel, you got a good snow-face-washing. Guess who got one? ☺

Finally it was time to eat. All our parents sat at the long table with their wives and husbands in the same spot they had sat in when they were children. All of us kids sat at a make-do table where we scrambled to sit next to our favorite cousins. Grandpa said the blessing which always was long because he mentioned each of our names that were present as well as the ones not with us. This included a lot of names, as there were twelve children in my mother's family that were alive and lived in different states. Grandpa even mentioned how he missed the ones that had died from an illness. When he finally said AMEN, he stood, and we passed our plates as he served the meat. All the rest of the food was passed around the table. There never was anything left over. What a wonderful meal!

When we gathered after dinner, there was singing, accompanied by an accordion and a violin. Then we went out to play again in the snow with our new mittens Grandma knitted. Us kids got mittens, and adults all got scarves. Before we went to bed, we all had a bowl of pudding. We anxiously waited to see who had the almond nut in their bowl, which would bring them good luck. Everyone cheered the winner, and he read *The Night Before Christmas*.

Before we went to bed, we had a cardamom roll with butter that was made while we were singing and a sweet hot drink. Grandpa read the Bible to us and said a prayer that included everyone. Grandpa and Grandma stood besides the stairs and hugged and kissed each one of us as we walked upstairs to our room. We went to sleep pretty fast, but all our folks were drinking that hot cinnamon-smelling drink I found out later was *GLOGG*. They told stories and laughed way into the night.

The next thing I remember was the sun shining brightly through the window and the smell of cardamom rolls, bread, and coffee. We scrambled

downstairs in our pajamas, sat as close as we could to the coal stove in the kitchen to keep warm, and ate our cardamom rolls with butter and jam. Mmmm! What wonderful memories of my first Christmas as a child!

A Special Christmas Memory

About sixty-five years ago my parents and I drove to my grandparents' home in the coal mining town of Byrnedale, Pennsylvania. It was so much fun to be a coal miner's granddaughter. I felt very special, as I was the only one in my grade at school. I promised my teacher I would tell the class all about the coal mining town the first day back at school when we shared our stories of Christmas Day.

I didn't think we would ever get there, as it snowed from the time we left our fourteenth-floor apartment in the city, till the time we finally drove off the two-lane tarmac highway onto the one-lane dirt road that led to the one-street town with houses on both sides of the street. I knew we were close by because just as we drove around the side of the mountain, I could see the bell in the steeple of the church. I vividly remember the day the bell arrived. The town people were very proud of it, as they all chipped in to buy it, and it had to come "from afar off." The day it arrived the whole town watched as it was put in place. Then everyone stopped. They listened eagerly as the oldest boy in the one-room schoolhouse pulled on the rope three times. Everyone cheered. Every time I visited my grandmother, she would tell me what a thrill it was the day when the bell rang three times. She said that it was sweet music to the ears of everyone.

This special Christmas we slowly passed the livery stable on the right. The town store was on the left. At the other end of the road, the coal mine was on the left and the saloon on the right. At the very end of the road between the coal mine and the saloon, sitting back in the trees, was the church.

I was really getting excited now. We had to pull off the road to make room for horses to go by. We finally drove up beside my grandparents' house. All the houses looked alike, except my grandparents' house had two rocking chairs on the porch, one for Grandmother Hilma and one for Great Grandmother

Kalgren. They sat in those chairs no matter what the weather. They called them their "knitting chairs" and that is actually what they did winter, spring, summer, and fall. The snow was about four feet plus high, but a place was shoveled out for our car, as well as a path to the door of the house, the outdoor john, the barn, and down to the creek where they cut out blocks of ice to store in the barn to use during the hot summer months. Hay covered the ice to keep it from melting. It was fun to play in that barn with my cousins, as we slid and jumped from one slippery block of ice to another slippery block of ice. Many times I lost my balance and fell. Whew, did I ever have black and blue marks!

My four-foot-seven, silver-white-haired grandmother, who tied her hair up in a bun at the back of her head, was right there with the door open to hug and kiss us. She never did pronounce Joanie just right. She pronounced my name "Yoanie." I ran into every room of the house on the first floor and didn't see a Christmas tree. Then I ran up the steps two at a time and looked in every room. I couldn't believe it! No Christmas tree was anywhere. My eyes filled with tears as I hopped and skipped two steps down at a time to tell my mother and dad. They told me not to worry, as I would see it soon enough. They hugged me and said that on Christmas morning when I woke up there would be a tree. I was puzzled, but now the smell of cardamom rolls baking took over and I realized I was hungry. The door opened and my six-foot-seven grandpa leaned down so he could come in the house. My mother and I ran to him to brush the snow off his clothes. His mustache was even covered with snow! He kissed and hugged my mother. Then as he shook my dad's hand, he bent down, lifted me up, and tickled my cheeks with his snowy mustache. Everyone was laughing as he danced around the room with me in his arms. Grandma joined him, and the three of us danced around the room. My mother and dad poured coffee and milk, set out the rolls, cheese, butter, and jam. The mouth-watering smell of cardamom seemed to reach all our nostrils at the same time, and we all sat down on the wooden benches alongside the table for a feast. I sat on my grandpa's lap. After all, I was his coal miner's granddaughter!

It was getting dark now, and Grandpa said, "Shh! Listen! This is welcoming you to our home and town." The bell in the steeple rang three times. Then

Grandpa started singing this familiar tune, and we all joined him. I fell asleep in his lap, and before I knew it, it was Christmas morning. I clamored down the stairs as fast as I could. Just as I hit the landing, I saw the Christmas tree with all its trimmings, and I heard the bell in the steeple ring three times.

I HEARD THE BELLS ON CHRISTMAS DAY

Henry Wadsworth Longfellow   1864

I heard the bells on Christmas day
Their old familiar carols play,
And wild and sweet the words repeat
Of peace on earth, good will to men.
And thought how, as the day had come,
The belfries of all Christendom
Had rolled along the unbroken song
Of peace on earth, good will to men.
Till ringing, singing on its way
The world revolved from night to day,
A voice, a chime, a chant sublime
Of peace on earth, good will to men.
And in despair I bowed my head
"There is no peace on earth," I said,
For hate is strong and mocks the song
Of peace on earth, good will to men."
Then pealed the bells more loud and deep:
"God is not dead, nor doth He sleep;
the wrong shall fail, the right prevail
with peace on earth, good will to men."

Christmas Taffy Pull

Christmas was always fun and exciting at the home of my grandparents in Byrnedale, Pennsylvania. Byrnedale was a coal mining town. I was always proud to be a coal miner's granddaughter, even though some older children wanted to hide that they were grandchildren of a coal miner. Not me. First, there was the excitement of packing the one-seater Ford coupe to get there. We three got up early to leave, so we could get out of the city before the trolleys started running. We packed our car with groceries from the local market. Mother had a couple crates of fruit. Dad always brought a cooked ham and a leg of roast lamb from the restaurant. The Italian family that lived on the seventh floor always gave us some fish from their family-owned fish market. The Greek family that lived on the first floor gave us a box of pastries they had made. The Polish family on the ninth floor gave us a long roll of their hot sausages. My aunts and uncles always came by at the last minute to wish us good luck and to add more Christmas presents into the car. Our small coupe was packed to capacity.

It had been snowing all night, and housewives and their older children were shoveling snow out of the street. School age children were shoveling snow off sidewalks. Some kids got up early, so they would have plenty of snow to build large forts. Younger kids made snowballs to go in the forts. By noon everyone was divided into teams, and they stood behind the forts at their apartment building. One person was chosen before lunch to stand on the roof and blow the whistle to start. The game lasted till the last snowball was thrown. We didn't get to see much of it as we were now out of the city and on the two-lane road going toward Grandma's house.

My dad, mother and I occupied the front seat of our car. Dad drove. Mother sat in the middle, so I would not aggravate Dad too much. I sat beside the window. We lived in Dearborn, Henry Ford's town. It was not unusual for us to see new cars in every color, make, size, and shape. But for the folks back in the coal mining town where my grandparents lived, it was exciting for them to have visitors who actually owned a car, let alone a car that was not black. Ours was green. Everyone in that town dropped by to look at it!

After several hours of driving, we were on the one lane road. It was so narrow that you pulled one side of your car off the road, and the other driver coming toward you did the same. Both cars drove quite slowly, with two tires of each car off the road. The drivers waved and shouted a greeting. Sometimes both drivers stopped and they talked to each other. Each driver told what to look out for and what was ahead. The only time we stopped was to get gas and go to the restroom. Gas stations were few and far between. Mother packed us sandwiches that we ate in the car. We always carried water in rinsed-out milk bottles from home. Once we had to use some of our drinking water to pour into the radiator. When Dad took the cap off the radiator, it went "Poof!" and steam burst out of it. He always said it was my good drinking water he poured in the radiator that stopped the steam. I always was happy when this happened, as I could get out of the car and run around for a while.

It was getting late now and dark outside. Mother couldn't read anymore, and I usually fell asleep by this time. Dad and I both loved Mom reading to us when we were driving somewhere. We were now off the tarmac and on a dirt road, which was a good sign. I woke up a little from time to time and asked how much longer it would take to get to Grandma's. When the answer was "over an hour," I knew Dad was teasing because within a few minutes we pulled off the dirt road and drove up beside Grandma's house. Then the excitement began, as everyone came out of the house surrounding our car with many questions, hugs, and kisses. Grandpa always picked me up and twirled me around and around. By this time we were glad to get in the house and warm our hands in front of the wood potbellied stove. It was so much fun seeing Grandpa and Grandma, cousins, aunts, and uncles. After all the presents and food were brought in, we were all called to the table for a feast of homemade cardamom rolls with butter, soup, and cookies with milk. No one stopped talking, but gradually we were fading, and Grandpa and Grandma walked all of us grandchildren to the staircase and kissed and hugged each one of us. We all said that we were not tired, but within ten minutes everything was quiet.

The next thing I knew someone was calling my name. It was morning. The sun was brightly shining. I hurried downstairs for a cardamom roll and jelly with a big glass of milk. Then all of us couldn't get dressed and out of the house soon enough. It was time to make taffy. "Hooray!" everyone shouted. "Who wants to make taffy?"

"I do! I do! I do!"

We knew how to make taffy outside in the winter. The snow was up to some of our waists and higher up for some of the little ones. Fresh snow had fallen through the night, and that made it even better. Grandma read the ingredients to us. All of us were excited, as everything she made was delicious. Grandma gave everyone something to do to get the taffy ready. Grandpa had logs piled up so that everything could be set on them. This is Grandma's recipe for *Christmas Taffy.*

Ingredients:
2 ½ cups white sugar or 2 ¼ cups packed brown sugar
1 ½ cups molasses or light corn syrup
4 teaspoons vinegar
Big pinch of salt
½ cup milk or leftover cream (or evaporated milk)

Preparation:
First, make white sugar taffy, then brown sugar taffy. To make brown sugar taffy, use just a little less than 2 1/2 cups of packed brown sugar instead of white sugar.

Mix all ingredients except the milk or cream in a big heavy pot.

Stir often until the sugar is completely dissolved. Increase the heat, but remember that the pot will get very hot; bring the mixture to boiling. VERY slowly add the milk or cream in a thin stream so the boiling does not stop.

Put candy thermometer in pan, and continue stirring. Cook and stir constantly until the mixture reaches 248° (firm ball stage). Dip a straw or pastry brush in water and gently brush the sides of the pot to wash the crystals from the sides of the pot. Do this a few times while the taffy is cooking. When the taffy has reached desired temperature, remove from the heat, remove thermometer and WITHOUT scraping the sides and bottom of the pot, pour mixture onto a large platter that has been greased with margarine or butter, or on top of new, freshly fallen snow where no person or creature has soiled the clean snow. Grease your hands with margarine or butter, and by this time the taffy should be cool enough to handle. Take a small portion of the taffy and begin pulling. Use only the tips of your fingers to pull. When pulled until cool and creamy or white in color, pull each strip slightly and place on waxed paper. Cut each strip into 1-inch pieces, and wrap each piece in a small piece of waxed paper and twist the ends. Store in a container with a tight fitting cover.

At Grandma's, every one chose a partner and pulled, laughed and laughed, pulled and pulled, and laughed till we fell on the snow exhausted. Some could twist better than others! The taffy no longer felt sticky when it was pulled enough and it was white or creamy in color. We twisted each pulled strip a little and placed it back on the snow. When all the taffy was pulled, we cut it to the size of our thumbs. We couldn't help but sneak some to eat. We were supposed to save it till Christmas day, but our sticky hands and faces gave us away. It is so much fun! We bragged all evening about who was the best twister. Just like the fish stories you hear, the fish that got caught was bigger and bigger the more times it was told. Before you knew it, some could twist longer than their arm! ☺ What a fun-filled day making and pulling taffy!

Eating Popcorn Balls

What is so special about eating popcorn balls? Do you know how they are made? Everything my grandmother made smelled so good! She was always kind to tell us her recipes and show us how to make delicious food to eat.

My grandmother made popcorn balls using a pinch of salt, not quite a half-cup of butter, and not quite a cup of corn syrup. She really mixed this with an oiled wooden spoon. Then she added a whole cup of sugar and a drop of vanilla after it was all stirred. Next, she poured the mixture in an iron kettle and let it bubble and boil. After it cooked awhile, she added another drop of vanilla. Then she took the popcorn off the wood stove and out of the iron kettle. She poured the hot syrup over the popcorn a little at a time, stirring constantly, until all the popcorn was coated. She set the popcorn outside to get cool. By the time she'd greased her hands with butter, the popcorn was cool and she could form it into balls. We could hardly wait to eat one of the popcorn balls! But we had to wait until they were tied to the bottom branches of the tall balsam Christmas tree. The tree smelled good too, especially when we were on our backs underneath the branches where our popcorn balls were tied. The candles on the tree were lit.

Everyone was seated while Grandpa first read from the Bible. After that he read a Christmas story from his worn out children's book he brought with him when he came to this country as a young man. It was delightful to listen to Grandpa read. He had an accent, but he would add words as he read and make us all laugh. When Grandpa finished, the girls scooted on their backs to lie flat under their favorite popcorn ball. When we were all comfy and in our place, the boys wiggled and grunted, but finally managed to shift themselves to lie flat under the popcorn ball they had been eyeing while Grandpa read. Then with a smile, Grandpa told us the rules. There were three rules to follow when you were eating. One was that you could not touch the popcorn ball with your hands. The second was that you could not change places with someone else. The third and the last rule was that the first one finished would be given their choice of which person they wanted to sit by at the table that evening.

Everything looked so different on your back on the floor looking up at the Christmas tree. Usually we sat on the floor to open presents and looked at the tree, or we stood looking up and down at it. There were never enough chairs for everyone, so I scooted up, leaned against the wall, sat down on the floor, and crisscrossed my legs. Now I was actually under the big, floor-to-ceiling balsam Christmas tree. Oh, it smelled so good! Candlelight glowed through the branches. It highlighted different areas of the center of the tree. A ray of light glowed on the curl of the girl next to me. Then I noticed a little stream of light flickering on the kernels of the popcorn ball next to me. I felt cozy and secure. To me, the whole world was wrapped up in the branches of that tree. I could even smell the tree when I first opened the door.

Grandpa gave the signal to start eating our popcorn balls; he could whistle true birdcalls. Then the excitement began. Giggles, ohhs, ahhs, grunts and groans, and most of all licking and slurping noises, filled the room. We tried to sink a couple of teeth into the sticky, gooey popcorn ball. Then we were on our way to devouring it more quickly. Some of us used our elbows for leverage. Usually within five minutes or so we were able to get some pretty good licking down. Determination followed once we got a taste of the sweet coating. Everyone cheered us on. The first one to win was the neighbor boy next door. I don't know how he did it, but he did. Eventually we all conquered our popcorn balls with a little help. What a mess everyone was, but we had so much fun. Next we took turns washing our faces and hands, and helping each other get the gooey stuff out of our hair.

We were called back to our Christmas tree to enjoy the rest of the evening with singing, quoting psalms, and listening to many fun tales of years gone by. Fifteen minutes before we went upstairs to bed was a silent time. We listened to music from the accordion and violin our uncles played, and we looked at our lovely Christmas tree that still today holds so many treasured memories.

Wax Candles on the Christmas Tree

It was Christmas Eve in Byrnedale, Pennsylvania, the coal mining town where my grandparents lived in the seventh house down from the coal mine. My cousins and I sat on the floor. We talked a mile a minute to tell each other what had been going on in our lives. One always tried to do one better than the others. It seemed like the younger ones exaggerated the most. When that happened, we all laughed. Sometimes they backed down, but not always. It was always so much fun to get together. All of us were from the city, so coming to visit our grandparents was a delight. We arrived all happy and jubilant. Leaving was another scene. We didn't like to leave, and everyone was crying, kissing, hugging, and promising to come back soon.

After we had our dinner, it wasn't long before we got sleepy. Gradually we were on our backs under the branches of the floor-to-ceiling Christmas tree. We talked for a while, but soon everyone got rather quiet, and we floated into dreamland. We took turns counting how many candles were on the tree. When our grandpa asked us, it seemed everyone had a different answer. The one that had the correct answer got to choose whom he wanted to sit next to at the breakfast table. Their choice was always Grandpa or Grandma.

There were basic rules when you were lying under the branches. You could not touch the candles, put your hand above a lit candle, or bump the branches. Grandpa made figures on the wall with his hands. We had to guess what the object was and whether it flew, walked, galloped, or hopped. We sang Christmas carols. First Grandpa and Grandma sang in Swedish. Oh, how we all loved to hear them sing! Then we took turns singing. Our uncles and aunts loved to sing, and they could harmonize. One of the uncles sang a solo, *Silent Night*. He asked everyone to join him on the last verse. When it was the cousins' turns, it was hilarious because some would make up the words when they couldn't remember them. If we didn't get too rowdy, we were allowed to stay under the tree longer, which we all loved to do, and listen to adult conversations going on.

Some fell asleep, but I pretended I was a queen, and visited all the homes on the street and blessed them with my special golden wand that lit up the minute I knocked on their doors. When they answered, I blessed them, and they received a very special present from the queen. Then my mother knelt down and touched my cheek. One by one we all went upstairs where we slept horizontal on the bed. The girls were in one bed, and the boys in another bed over by the other wall.

There was something special about watching the glow of homemade wax candles on the Christmas tree. Everything seemed peaceful and safe. We had not a care in the world. Candles cracked, and the wax dripped out on the branches. The wax looked like snow on the branches. Sometimes the wax dropped down to the floor. This wasn't good, but fortunately it didn't burn anyone.

As we went to sleep, it felt good that tomorrow Grandpa was going to take us way down into the mine. One at a time he let us lie on his back as he steered the four-wheel wagon. It was scary as we went down so far, and it got dark. We walked back up, and gradually we saw the light from the opening get brighter and brighter. Walking back up was very strenuous, and we were glad to get back to the house to lie down under the branches of the tree. The wax candles wouldn't be lit till it got dark, and some of us fell asleep waiting, but before we knew it, we were called to the table for a feast.

When we were excused from the table, we all lay down in the same place as the night before under the branches of the Christmas tree. Grandpa came in to light the wax candles. We talked about what we saw when we went far down into the coal mine. Grandpa always said that if we had actually gone down as far as we thought we did, we would be in China. Was there magic in the glow of wax candles on the Christmas tree? No one ever seemed to talk so much as when we were under the tree. We were in our own comfortable, safe zone, and each of us entered our very own dreamland. The glow from the candles took over, and life seemed very good. It couldn't be better. I don't know about the others, but I dreamed that I was queen again and again. That was the magic in the glow of the wax candles for me.

Christmas at a Frontier Pastor's House

Singing was a vital tradition in our family, along with fun and inspiring stories that have shaped my life and made me who I am. When you consider my parents' living in a coal miner's town where employers provided the houses with no toilet facilities, running water or electricity, one could think how unfortunate those people were to live such an impoverished life. But it was a rich life, filled with love that could not be bought. It was filled with stories of grandparents coming over from the old country and settling in a coal mining town with immigrants from all over the world. Not a family came to work and settle that my grandfather couldn't converse with in their own language. I am blessed with a rich inheritance of godly, loving grandparents who accepted me as one of their own even though I myself was born in a shack without electricity and water to a mother who was not married, yet loved me from day one. I like the following story, *Christmas at a Frontier Pastor's House*, because it mirrors my growing up years. It gives me comfort to know that Our Heavenly Father, who owns the cattle on a thousand hills, the wealth in every mine, will care for me. My mother was the best reader in our family, and this was one of my favorite stories of all that she read to me.

Christmas at a Frontier Pastor's House

I remember a day one winter that stands out like a boulder in my life. The weather was unusually cold, our salary had not been regularly paid, and it did not meet our needs when it was.

My husband was away much of the time, traveling from one district to another. Our boys were well, but my little Ruth was ailing, and at last none of us were decently clothed. I patched and re-patched, with spirits sinking to the lowest ebb. The water gave out in the well, and the wind blew through the cracks in the floor.

The people in the parish were kind, and generous too, but the settlement was new, and each family was struggling for itself. Little by little, at the time I needed it most, my faith began to waiver. Early in life I was taught to take God at His word, and I thought my lesson was well learned. I had leaned upon the promises in dark times, until I knew as David did, "who was my fortress and my deliverer." Now a daily prayer for forgiveness was all that I could offer. My husband's coat was hardly thick enough for October, and he was often obliged to ride miles to attend some meeting or funeral. Many times our breakfast was Indian cake (corn bread) and a cup of tea without sugar.

Christmas was coming. The children always expected their presents. I remember the ice was thick and smooth, and the boys were craving a pair of skates. Ruth, in some unaccountable way, had taken a fancy that the dolls I had made were no longer suitable. She wanted a nice large one, and insisted on praying for it.

I knew it seemed impossible, but oh, I wanted to give each child its present. It seemed as if God had deserted us, but I did not tell my husband all this. He worked so earnestly and heartily. I supposed him to be as hopeful as ever. I kept the sitting room cheerful with an open fire, and I tried to serve our scanty meals as invitingly as I could. The morning before Christmas, James was called to see a sick man.

I put a piece of bread for his lunch. It was the best I could do. I wrapped my plaid shawl around his neck and then tried to whisper a promise as I often had, but the words died away upon my lips. I let him go without it.

That was a dark, hopeless day. I coaxed the children to bed early for I could not bear their talk when Ruth went to bed. I listened to her prayer. She asked for the last time most explicitly for her doll and for skates for her brothers. Her bright face looked so lively when she whispered to me, "You know, I think they'll be here early in the morning, mamma." I sat down alone, and gave way to the bitterest tears.

Before long James returned, chilled and exhausted. He took off his boots. The thin stockings slipped off with them, and his feet were red with cold. I wouldn't treat a dog that way, let alone a faithful servant," I said. Then as I glanced up and saw the hard lines in his face, and the look of despair, it flashed across to me - James had let go too. I brought him a cup of tea, feeling sick and dizzy at the very thought. He took my hand and we sat for an hour without a word. I wanted to die and to meet God, and tell Him His promises were not true; my soul was so full of rebellious despair.

There came a sound of bells, a quick stop, and a loud knock at the door. James sprang up to open it. There stood Deacon White. "A box came by express just before dark. I brought it around as soon as I could get away. Reckon it might be for Christmas. At any rate, I said they shall have it tonight. Here is a turkey my wife asked me to fetch along, and these other things I believe belong to you."

There was a basket of potatoes, and a bag of flour. Talking all the time, he hurried in the box, and then with a hearty good night he rode away. Still without speaking, James found a chisel and opened the box. He drew out first a red blanket, and then we saw that beneath it, the box was full of clothing. It seemed at that moment as if Christ fastened upon me a look of reproach. James sat down and covered his face with his hands, "I can't touch them." He exclaimed, "I haven't been true, just when God was trying me to see if I could hold out. Do you think I could not see how you were suffering?" I had no word of comfort to offer. I know now how to preach the awfulness of turning away from God."

"James," I said clinging to him, "don't take it to heart like this. I am to blame. I ought to have helped you. We will ask him together to forgive us."

"Wait a moment dear, I can't talk now," he said. Then he went into another room. I knelt down, and my heart broke. In an instant all the darkness, all the stubbornness rolled away. Jesus came again and stood before me, with the loving word, "Daughter!" and sweet promises of tenderness and joy of soul. I was so lost in praise and gratitude that I forgot anything else. I don't know how long it was before James came back, but he too had found peace. "Now my dear wife," he said, "let us thank God together." And he then poured out words of praise, Bible words for nothing else could express our thanksgiving.

It was 11 o'clock, the fire was low and there was the great box, and nothing touched but the warm blanket we needed. We piled on some fresh logs, lighted two candles, and began to examine our treasure. We drew out an overcoat. I made James put it on; just the right size, and I danced around him. Then there was a cloak, and he insisted on seeing me in it. My spirits always affected him, and we both laughed like foolish children. There was a warm suit of clothes also and three pairs of woolen hose. There was a dress for me, yards of flannel, a pair of arctic overshoes for each of us. In mine was a slip of paper. I have it now and mean to hand it down to my children. It was Jacob's blessing to Asher, "Thy shoes shall be iron and brass, and as the days, so shall thy strength be." In the gloves, evidently for James, the same dear hand had written, "I the Lord thy God will hold thy right hand, saying unto thee, Fear not, I will help thee."

It was a wonderful box, and packed with thoughtful care. There was a suit of clothes for each of the boys, and a little red gown for Ruth. There were mittens, scarves, and hoods. Down in the center of the box was another box. We opened it and there was a great wax doll. I burst into tears again. James wept for joy. It was too much. We then both exclaimed again. Close behind it came two pair of skates. There were books for us to read, some of them I had wished to see, stories for the children to read, aprons and underclothing, knots of ribbon, a lovely photograph, needles, buttons, thread and actually a muff, and an envelope containing a ten-dollar gold piece. At last we cried over everything we took up.

It was past midnight, and we were faint and exhausted even with happiness. I made a cup of tea and cut a fresh loaf of bread, and James boiled some eggs. We drew up the table before the fire. How we enjoyed our supper! And then we sat talking over our life and how sure a help God always proved.

You should have seen the children the next morning. The boys raised a shout at the sight of their skates. Ruth caught up her doll and hugged it tightly without a word. Then she went to her room and knelt by her bed. When she came back she whispered to me, "I knew they would be there, Mamma, but I wanted to thank God just the same. We went to the window, and there were the boys out of the house already and skating on the ice with all their might.

My husband and I tried to return thanks to the church in the East that sent us the box and have tried to give thanks to God everyday since. Hard times have come again and again, but we have trusted Him, dreading nothing so much as a doubt of His protecting care. Over and over again we have proved that "they that seek the Lord shall not want anything."

Aunt Emma and Mom

Joanie

Chef Dean, my dad

CHAPTER 3

INHERITED CHARACTER

Photo Essay

Here I am holding the branch of a tree with shiny leaves in the summer. I am three years old with a crop of short, curly bright-red hair, a sleeveless one-piece flowered cotton suit with a wide-buttoned belt on, and high-top, glossy, laced shoes, still wondering why I have to smile while clinging to that tree branch. My Aunt Emma is still calling me Joanie when my name is Rosemarie, and she wants me to smile so she can take a picture of me to surprise my mother on her birthday.

This picture seemed to me like it was taking an awfully long time, and now I could feel my nose getting spots of water on it, plus I was very uncomfortable. Aunt Emma assured me it would only be a few more minutes and that my perspiration would go away soon. Whatever perspiration was, I wanted to get rid of it, have this picture taken, and get away from holding the branch which was making my hand wet too.

I wasn't so well liked, taking so long holding this tree branch. My Aunt Emma was not letting other kids get near the tree, and it was the only tree for many blocks. We lived in an apartment building on the 14th floor. It was: whoever got to the tree first, could play there. Many, many times we stood in line not only to crowd around the tree and play, but also to dig in the dirt around the tree with the spoons we brought from our mother's kitchen. That little patch was the only dirt around the apartment. The sidewalk stretched from the brick apartment building to the street curb. If you wanted grass and a sandbox, you had to be taken to one of the city parks which was fun, but not very close to where we lived. Mothers took turns sometimes, and I got to go with them to the city park. It usually was during the time when it was my mother's turn to wash clothes in the basement. I really wanted to help my mother wash clothes, as it looked like a lot of fun, but the landlord didn't like children around the wringer washing machines, as there had been accidents. He was an old crabby Italian guy who barely spoke English.

Finally my aunt snapped the picture. The kids hollered and hooped with glee, charged toward the tree, and fought to hold the branch. Wow! Was I ever glad that was over!

My Aunt Emma was still calling me Joanie, but at this point I didn't care what she called me, as all I wanted to do was dig in the dirt and see how many spoonfuls I could dig out. I was always told if you dug deep enough you would reach China.

Grandpa Lundgren

Arvid Carl was my grandpa Lundgren. Oh, how I loved him! He always had time for me. He came over from the "ole country", as he called it, with his older brother, Erik. There wasn't any question that he was a Swede and loved by all. When they arrived in America, they were taken to Duluth, Minnesota. They worked on farms for a place to sleep and eat. Grandpa would preach when the preacher was called away. Erik fell in love with Hilma Kalgren, who lived with her mother. She took in laundry to make ends meet. One Sunday the preacher introduced Grandpa and Uncle Erik to his uncle who was visiting from Pennsylvania. He told them there were jobs at the coal mine. Erik could now marry Hilma. Hilma and her mother agreed to go with them to where Erik and Grandpa could get jobs. The mine provided a house for them. Grandpa spoke and wrote several languages, so he was the one who met the train when new families came to work at the coal mine. Yes, he was a coal miner along with his brother, Erik.

He said he would never be a fisherman. Too many people got sick on the ship coming over. All he could see was water and sky for weeks. He kept looking for land. When the ship docked, he was one of the first to walk off and set his feet on American soil. He didn't ever want to go fishing or get in a boat of any kind again. He loved what he called good dirt, where you could plant potatoes, vegetables, and flowers. All they'd had to eat on the ship was salted fish with hard bread. The last week on the ship they ran out of water. "All the water in the ocean, and not a drop to drink," he said.

Grandpa had quite a limp, along with pain, which happened when he was climbing over a fence as a teenager. He was pushed by his brothers and broke his ankle. He never told his parents, as he did not want to get his brothers in trouble. He limped all his life. He was a handsome man. He was six foot seven in height, had brown wavy hair and sparkling brown eyes. He always had time to read to me, tell me stories of the "ole country" in Swedish and English, and give me many hugs and laughter. He was proud to be an American citizen. He recited parts of the Constitution to me and had a picture of the American flag on the wall in the dining room.

We had many family gatherings back in Pennsylvania. I loved that coal mining town. There was one road with houses on each side. At one end of the road was a coal mine off to the left, and to the right was the company store. Families charged everything they bought till the end of the month when the miners got paid. I walked down to the company store every day to ask if there was any mail for my grandpa and grandma from the "ole country". A little farther down from the company store was the saloon. People were always in the saloon. Most of them were men with a few women sitting with them. I used to peek in and wonder why they drank during the day, and why they weren't at work.

The other end of the road was the livery stable run by a local Indian who was the father of the wife of one of my uncles. He took us kids on sleigh rides and hayrides. He cleared a trail, and we rode one of his old mares. The trail wasn't very long. The mares were really ready for "la la land," but what fun we had riding them.

Around the bend in the midst of some trees stood the church Grandpa and his brother helped build. It had long benches inside, a stand on a platform for the preacher to place his Bible, and a real piano. The service was first in Swedish and then in English, with twenty minutes between services. Everyone stayed for both services. Parents wanted their children to keep up with the Swedish language, and parents needed to learn the English language.

There was an influenza epidemic and Uncle Erik got very sick and died. Grandpa promised him that he would take care of his wife and children. He married my Aunt Hilma, and she became my grandma. He always said that was the best way to take care of her and her children. Together, they added six more children to the family of six.

Sunday dinner was the best meal of the week. If we went to church, we could sit at the table and have dinner. If we did not go to church, we didn't sit at the table and have dinner. There were no exceptions to Grandpa's rule. It was very rare for anyone to miss church more than once.

I loved Sunday afternoons with Grandpa. He read to us, sang with us, and took us on walks up the mountain. When there was a baptism, he walked with us down to the creek. He carried me when I was afraid a snake was near a bush. He let me sit on his lap when he took a nap. He told me stories of my mother when she was a little girl. The only time we couldn't go with Grandpa was when he first came home from work. That was the time he took Grandma's hand, and they went for a walk no matter what the weather. Grandpa had to bend down when he walked with Grandma in order to hold her hand. She was only four feet eleven inches tall.

Grandpa passed away when I was in third grade. He taught me many things that have stayed with me all these years. He was proud to be an American. So am I. He loved reading from the Bible. So do I. He loved to sing. So do I. He was thankful for being able to work. So am I. He loved his home and family. So do I. He always welcomed families that emigrated from the "ole country". So do I. He made everyone feel at home when they dropped in for a chat. So do I. He loved going to church. So do I. He loved Sunday dinner. So do I.

Best of all, I loved my grandpa and he loved me.

Chef Dean

My dad was a chef. I was proud of him. From the day I started school in first grade until this day, I tell everyone that my dad was a chef. He could cook anything. You name it, and he would cook it for you. I ate every bowl of food he ever set before me. He always said a prayer, and if you were not thankful, you kept it a secret. I liked everything he made; I didn't always know what it was, but I liked it. After I ate it, he teased me and told me it was turtle soup, pig knuckles cut up in fried potatoes, or squirrel stew.

Many times I've been asked how my dad learned to cook and how he became a chef. He was from a family of sixteen. He was born and raised in the hills of Kentucky, and they were very poor. He always told me never to be discouraged when things didn't go right. He said his family planted seeds every year; some years their crop didn't produce enough to feed the family. This didn't stop the family prayers in the evenings or mornings. They were always thankful for another day to work in the fields and to sleep under a roof at night.

The boys had to leave home by the age of nine years old and the girls at twelve years old because there was not enough food to feed them. When one of them started walking down the road from home, his mother was always in tears. He wore two shirts, a pair of trousers and no socks. He carried his shoes because they didn't fit, and his mother gave him a loaf of bread. He woofed down that loaf of bread before noon, he was so hungry. He followed the road by the creek, and drank water with his hands for a cup. Toward evening on the second day, he saw in the distance a huge tent. As he walked toward it, he saw a big waste container and he started digging in it for something to eat. People in the make-to kitchen of the Barnum and Bailey Circus saw this tall, skinny tow-headed kid and took him in and fed him. He stayed with them about a year and worked in their kitchen. He washed dishes, pots and pans, carried out the garbage, burned the trash, swept out the stalls of the animals, cleaned the outdoor johns, and peeled and washed vegetables. He fed the animals all the scraps and carried up buckets of water for them to drink.

Because of his interest, they gradually taught him how to cook. He took to it right away, surprising them by adding this and that to make it taste better. He picked leaves, cut them up into small pieces and added them to soups. At first, they were aghast, but they let him do it. He took over-ripe apples from the ground and mashed them up and put them on some of the meat that was too dry. Old folks looked us up when I was a young girl and told mom and I stories about my dad and his cooking in the make-to tent at the circus.

Life was good and fun with my mom and dad. We were poor, but I didn't know it. Dad always worked, and by the time I was in high school and college, he worked in hotels as the chef. He was featured in a Southern magazine as the "Chef of Chefs." He taught my mother and all her sisters, his sisters and cousins by the dozens to cook. The women loved him because he did all the cooking for family reunions!

Do I cook? Sorry to say, no. Dad wanted to teach me many times, but I always told him that he was the very best chef in all the world, and why not live in the same town all our lives? It didn't quite work out that way, but I really wanted it to, and so did my dad, the very best chef in the world.

Dad and Mom at Breakfast

My dad left for work seven days a week no later than 4:30 a.m. Why so early? I remember these early morning conversations between my mom and dad every day of my life when I lived at home.

Mom felt they should have one meal together, so they agreed on an early breakfast, as lunch and dinner was not an option when dad was working. Mom prepared breakfast and set a nice table. They talked and once in a while some comment struck their funny bone and they laughed. As mom fixed breakfast, dad shaved. When they sat down at the table, dad asked how long she cooked the oatmeal, or did she flip the eggs after fifty seconds. If it was pancake Sunday, he asked how long it was before she turned the flapjacks. On and on it went. I thought it was a monotonous conversation.

Dad always thanked mom for the breakfast and carried the dishes over to the sink. Some mornings he walked out and cut an orange blossom off the tree in the back yard, or he picked guava leaves from one of our two guava trees, and put them in a little glass and made a cute arrangement. Everything went smoothly until he had to leave for work because mom wanted him to stay longer.

Dad's thoughts were already at his work place. He was nervous about getting all the ovens turned on, getting the meat out of the walk-in refrigerators, and checking to see if the potato peeler man arrived on time and was peeling the potatoes for the day. When the pastry baker came in, Dad said there was always a "shower of flour" all over the place when she emptied those fifty-pound bags of flour. I loved it when she emptied the bags as she gave the empty ones to me. They had colorful pictures on them, and my mother used the bags to sew something for me, our Toy Manchester dog, or for my stuffed animals.

Still at home though, my dad backed out of the garage, and my mother walked out to the alley and waved to Dad until the car was out of sight. Then she came into the house, cleaned up the dishes, and set the table for me. Mother always sat down with me while I had breakfast, and we talked about everything imaginable. Those were fun times, those early morning breakfast times, listening to Dad and Mom at the breakfast table and hearing them kiss "goodbye" and say how much they loved each other. And I knew it was my chance to be with Mom for breakfast, which always turned out to be fun.

Yellow

Several pictures come to my mind when I think of the color, yellow. It always gives me a smile when I see it displayed in pictures, in clothing, flowers, vegetables, fresh eggs cracked open and hitting hot sizzling butter in a fry pan, bananas hanging upside down on trees, corn boiling in a pot, and most importantly, in streams of sunlight bursting through skies after storms.

One of two of my mother's housedresses was bright and cheerful, predominantly the color yellow. She was blond, five-foot-eight inches tall, with brown eyes and olive skin. She was a beauty. All her favorite clothes had some yellow in them. Her winter coat was a fuzzy, wooly lemon-sherbet yellow.

One day at school, a rather thin, small boy ran down the street instead of standing in line with the rest of us in class. The boys said he had a yellow streak down his back, and they gave him such names as yellow-belly and yellow duck-feet. I felt sorry for him. We talked, and he read to me after school when everyone was gone. This young man who was so scared and had to put up with this cruel name-calling, turned out to be a captain in the fire department. He wore yellow safety gear when he spoke on SAFETY at the local schools in his hometown.

This song written by Stuart Hamblen in 1953 is a cheerful reminder of the beautiful yellow sunshine that makes us warm, cozy and comfy.

> So let the sunshine in
> Face it with a grin
> Smilers never lose
> And frowners never win
> So let the sunshine in
> Face it with a grin
> Open up your heart and let the sun shine in.

My Unique Aunt

What are the qualifications of a unique aunt? Just what makes an aunt unique? Is an aunt more unique if she is from your dad's side of the family, or from your mother's side of the family? Perhaps you would be a unique aunt if you were taller than the rest of the family, or if you were shorter than the rest of the family. Is an aunt unique if she has all of her own teeth, or if she has false teeth and uses Polident instead of Colgate Dental Cream? Is your aunt unique if she prefers riding a motorcycle, instead of driving a car? Is your aunt unique if she smokes a cigar, instead of a fashionable cigarette in a pearl holder?

Is your aunt unique if she drinks until the wee hours of Sunday morning, but she is always on time to teach Sunday school? Is your aunt unique if she walks home carrying two large bags of groceries to save the five cents it would cost her to ride the bus on ladies' day? Is your aunt unique if she has breakfast ready for her husband at 4:30 a.m., when he goes to work and hands him his lunch bucket as he walks out the door? Is an aunt unique if she bakes a coconut cake every Tuesday afternoon and invites all the children in the neighborhood to have a slice? Do you consider your aunt unique when you wake up on Sunday morning and she has all the shoes of the family polished and set next to their bedroom doors? Is your aunt unique if she washes, irons, and mends your clothes as well as the clothes of her family? Is your aunt unique if she always remembers your birthday? Is your aunt unique if she takes you along with her children on a boat ride? Is your aunt unique if she buys you your first watch?

The above qualities are just a few of those that make an aunt unique. I could name many more characteristics, and I could write the name of one of my aunts after each character quality. I have wonderful, unique aunts. I never visited, stayed overnight, talked to them on the phone, or received letters from them where they didn't tell me that they loved me. I want to be a unique aunt to my nephews and nieces, be there when they need me, and tell them that I love them "a bushel and a peck, and a hug around the neck".

My Uncles

I have been most fortunate to be part of a large family. My dad is from a family of sixteen, and my mother is from a family of twelve. I enjoyed every one of my uncles on both sides of the family. Even with occasional visits and family reunions, I never saw enough of them as a child.

In our travels every year to Central Florida, we visited Uncle Charlie. This was fun because they had a large orange grove. We picked and ate all the oranges we wanted. One year on the east coast of Florida we visited Uncle Roger who owned Dean's Chevrolet. This was fun because he gave us a ride in any new car on his lot. When we traveled through Kentucky, we visited Uncle Harlow. They grew tobacco and had a pig farm. I loved to climb up in the apple tree when it was loaded with apples in the fall and vigorously shake the tree. The pigs grunted and snorted and went after those apples when they fell to the ground. Tobacco, hanging row by row to dry out in the barns, was lovely. I never understood why some of the workers chewed it. Their house didn't have electricity. I loved sinking down into the feather bed at night, the glow of the kerosene lamp cozy and comfy.

Every other year we drove to Pennsylvania and New York to visit Uncle Clifford, Uncle Emil, and Uncle Walter. They told stories of the "good ole days". Uncle Walter always told us to eat as much as we wanted to, as it was paid for. This was unusual for most people, as everyone "owed the company store". Uncle Emil let us help him cut blocks of ice from the river. He stored them in the barn, covered with hay, so they would keep for use in the winter. Uncle Clifford took us on walks through the neighborhood called Swede Hill and told us stories about each family that came over from the old country. I had to listen carefully as those uncles had unusual accents. Oh, how those three laughed and got everyone else laughing!

We stopped in Ohio where I was born. Cuyahoga County was exciting to me, as I had five uncles who lived and worked there. Uncle Watt and Uncle Ed owned diners and were cooks like my dad. One of the diners had writing on the wall: *As you wander on through life whatever be your goal. Keep your eye upon the donut, and not upon the hole.* I thought this was funny! I read it to every customer who walked through the door. I have quoted it all my life. Uncle Herdis came in while we were there and told me that it was "positive thinking", and that I should always say it out loud when things didn't go just right. We didn't often get to see Titus, William, and George who worked in the brick factory.

Next we drove to Michigan, and usually stayed the summer where Dad was a chef in one of the big hotels. This was a paradise for me, as we would get together with many uncles, aunts, and cousins by the dozens on mostly my mother's side of the family. Every evening when the uncles came home from work we got together. The four uncles we saw most were Franz, Oscar, Ed, and Helmer. Uncle Oscar and Uncle Helmer were big, strapping men. Uncle Franz owned an ice cream store. Uncle Oscar was in the refrigeration business. Helmer owned his own milk delivery trucks. Uncle Ed worked for his sister's husband in the tool and die business. It was loads of fun being with them, as everyone sat outside on their small porch and front lawn. When the ice cream man came around, the uncles bought all of us ice cream bars. There were so many of us that we emptied his ice cream wagon. He always smiled, since he could then go home early after having sold everything.

Summer days went by too fast, and the time to go south came again too soon. We didn't make any stops going south as Dad was always in a hurry to find a job, find a place to live, and get me back in school. Oh, those wonderful hazy, lazy days of summer filled with loads of fun with all my uncles, aunts, and cousins by the dozens.

Do I have a favorite uncle? How could I? They were all so good to me. I always felt special when I was with them. They even listened to me practice my saxophone. I never felt I was very good, but they always clapped when I finished a selection, and they told me to keep practicing, as I was getting better and better every year. I loved every one of my twenty-eight uncles. Each has a special place in my heart.

Oranges and Strawberries

Aunt Sarah, my dad's oldest sister, and Uncle Charlie moved from Kentucky to Florida by mule train with their twelve children. They were the first in Aunt Sarah's family to move. Everyone thought they had lost their minds! When asked why they were moving, their answer was, "We're going to plant orange trees, and one of our daughters wants to have a strawberry farm." This is exactly what they did. Even though they had to quit school at an early age, they were exceptionally bright and gave God the glory for how He led them to go south with their family.

They bought a small house in Plant City, Florida with acreage and planted a grove of orange trees. They experimented in the grafting of their fruit trees, and to their amazement, the fruit trees began fruiting two years later. The results of their grafting attracted large companies, such as the Sunkist Growers, which was the largest marketing cooperative in the world's fruit industry.

When my dad, mom, and I visited them, they served us orange juice in the morning, and in the evening they boiled the leaves of the oranges to make tea. One of their sons took orange peels out to the garden as slug repellant; the ole slugs shriveled up. I loved mealtime, as Uncle Charlie prayed over the food and mentioned my name in the prayer.

One of their older daughters, Gracie, was my favorite cousin. One year when we came back, she was married. She and her husband bought a farm close by my aunt and uncle and planted strawberries. They had a large family. We stayed with them when it was strawberry-picking time in March and April. I loved that time of year. We all got up at the crack of dawn and picked strawberries, putting them in buckets to be washed. They took them to market the same day. To celebrate a plentiful strawberry harvest, every March the town commemorated with an 11-day festival called the Florida Strawberry Fesitval that ranks among the top 30 festivals in North America. This area has become the Winter Capital of the world.

When we got close to Plant City, my dad, mom, and I sang: "I want to wake up in the morning where the orange blossoms grow. Where the sun comes peeping into where I am sleeping and the songbirds say, *Hello*! I want to walk in the orange groves with my Aunt Sarah by my side and take an orange and squeeze the juice till I'm satisfied." Then Mom and Dad said to me, "Hug me, Joanie, and hug me quick! Hug me till my little heart ticks!"

A young family eventually bought out the strawberry plantation and made it a gold mine. It still produces the best strawberries I have ever eaten in the Winter Strawberry Capital of the World. After about ten years, my Aunt Sarah and Uncle Charlie were contacted and bought out by a large citrus company. They were given a fair, generous price, and the company agreed to let them live there the rest of their lives. The company never dreamed Aunt Sarah would live to be 106 years old. She was in good health till the day she went home to be with the Lord.

Up and Down the Haystacks

In all of our travels north, south, east and west for dad to find a job, one of my favorite fun places to go was my cousin's in Plant City, Florida near Dad's sister. It was so much fun because there was always a new haystack in the spring. For some reason, we were in that area at the time they were just starting to cut the hay, or else they had just finished, so we played sliding up and down till we were thoroughly exhausted. The minute we arrived at the farm, I jumped out of the car, hugged all my relatives, and headed to the haystacks as fast as my feet would carry me. My cousin always said to me and some other children, "Let's make hay while the sun shines." We answered, "Let's play with the hay while the sun shines."

Sometimes a small haystack was in the barn where we climbed up on the rafters and slid down. We drew straws to see who could slide down first, but before we did anything one of the hired help looked for snakes with his pitchfork. This was a little scary for me. Sometimes he found a curled-up snake, but he managed to curl it on his pitchfork and carry it away. I asked the farmer, "Why do snakes like it in the haystacks in here where it's dark and cool?" He looked me right in the eye and said, "That is why they like it. Don't worry, Joanie. I'll find them if they are here and take them out."

We played sliding up and down the haystack in the barn till we were called for supper. We went to the water pump outside and washed our hands and threw handfuls of water on everyone. None of us escaped getting drenched, but it felt so good. One of my cousins said a prayer at the table, and we had a delicious fried squirrel dinner. I thought it was chicken, and when I found out what it was, I was shocked. I didn't think people ate squirrels, but I was wrong. I thought they were teasing me. I whispered in my dad's ear later, and he said it was squirrel.

We were not excused from the table till everyone had finished their dinner, so it didn't do me any good to eat as fast as I could swallow. When we were finally excused, all of us made a beeline to the door and went right down to the outdoor haystack. They had a ladder rigged up to the side, so we could reach the top. The top was rounded off so we could sit and put our hands to the side in the straw and give ourselves a push. Down we went and within seconds we were skidding on the ground. We went up and down dozens of times till we were called to come in the house. Even though we didn't want to stop, we knew were tired and ready for bed.

All the adults sat on the sofa and chairs, and the rest of us leaned against their legs or stretched out on the floor. They read the Bible to us, and the next thing I knew, my mom whispered in my ear that it was time to go to bed. I don't remember one thing when I went to bed till the next morning when I smelled homemade bread from the kitchen.

Don't Sit Under the Apple Tree

My cousin, the daughter of my dad's sister, lived in the hills of Kentucky. She worked in a one-room post office for more than 30 years in Olive Hill, Kentucky. It was her dad's job, but as he got older his eyesight was dimming, and she helped him out. She had a terrific sense of humor, and when I was with her I always had so much fun. She was a terrific cook. She grew vegetables in her garden that could have been sent in to our cuisine magazines. A fenced-in area around her apple tree was home for her snorting pigs. I slept in a feather bed, and when I crawled into it, I slithered way down so low no one could see me. It was very comfy. She had a kerosene lamp on the dresser that produced a lovely glow on the walls and ceiling of the room. I was so comfortable I thought I was in heaven.

I was interested in stamps, especially the history behind each one. This cousin started me saving stamps in a small black book. The farmer's wives cut cancelled stamps off their packages and gave them to her, and she mailed them to me. I really enjoyed my collection of stamps from her. It cost three cents in those days to mail a letter, and the postman delivered mail both in the morning and in the afternoon.

One time my dad and mom left me with my cousin for a few days, as dad was interested in getting a job in the big city close by. I followed my cousin everywhere. My job was to shake apples off the apple tree so the pigs could eat the apples. I climbed up in the tree. At first, I pulled apples off and threw them down to the pigs, but then I thought of a better way. I started shaking furiously one branch at a time. This worked quite well. The pigs snorted and made lots of noise as they slurped down the apples. I liked the apples also, so I sat on a branch and started munching apples. My cousin called to me not to eat too many, as I would get a tummy ache. I should have taken her advice, as I did have a tummy ache during the night.

Getting down from the tree branches was quite a challenge. I didn't want to sit or stand under the apple tree with the pigs, even though they were harmless. I felt quite intimidated. Gradually I got down and stood with them. I sat down next to a couple pigs and found them quite friendly. Everyone laughed when they saw me. I was tired and they helped me up. I said to them as I turned around and walked to the house, "Don't sit under the apple tree with anyone else but me!" We all laughed.

Three Favorite Places to Swim

I wanted to learn to swim so badly. We were visiting my Grandma Lundgren in Byrnedale, Pennsylvania, and my cousins there could swim. We were down at the creek right by the railroad tracks. My mom and dad couldn't swim, so a couple of my cousins who knew how to swim said they'd teach me down at the creek, so my folks agreed and said they'd walk down to the creek and watch.

I ran on down happily with my cousins and a couple of their friends; my folks slowly walked down to the creek. It was a nice warm day, and we all had our makeshift swimsuits on. My cousins didn't wait for my folks to come to teach me. They jumped right in and had to paddle a little because the water was over their heads. One of my cousins hollered to me to jump in over here, and he pointed to a tree. I was too nervous and scared to jump, but one of the kids pushed me, and kerplunk, I was in over my head gasping for breath and gulping down water. They hollered at me to start splashing, and one of them threw me a branch to hold on to. My folks were petrified and not happy, but I was doing fine as long as I had that small branch to hold on to.

My next swim was in the Gulf of Mexico at the St. Pete Beach in St. Petersburg, Florida. We took the trolley that was a block from our house back and forth to the beach. That beach has smooth, white sand and warm Gulf of Mexico water. Sometimes we stayed late and saw unbelievable, incredible sunsets. We could hardly wait to walk on the beach, get sand between our toes, and jump the salty waves. We really didn't swim even though we tried because the waves kept knocking us off our feet.

My third favorite swimming hole was Weeki Wachee Springs, the "City of Mermaids", in Weeki Wachee, Florida. It was a swamp when I was young, and my folks watched me as I paddled myself around. I told them I could see for miles, and they just smiled. I'd say, "I really can!" We would be living a different lifestyle if they had taken me seriously. We went back a couple of years later. They had an underwater theater, and men and women dressed as mermaids performed. One of their favorite shows was *The Little Mermaid*. The last time I was there, they let me hold on to their mermaid tails and swim around with them. I couldn't hold my breath for two minutes like they could, so they brought me to the surface after 45 seconds or so. I had a lot of fun with the mermaids when we went to Florida a couple of times a year where dad always got a job not far from Weeki Wachee Springs. One of the mermaids' sayings was:

> We're not like other women. We don't have to clean an oven.
> And we will never grow old.
> We've got the whole world by the tail!

Influential People

Many times I heard Jackie Gleason say, "How Great It Is!" I can say, "How Great It Is" in my life too because of the many people who influenced me in making decisions. Some were for the better, and some not for the better.

My dad encouraged me all the time. He said, "Go for it, Joanie, and do your very best. If you don't do well, try something else." My folks planted a garden every year. Sometimes the crops did well, and sometimes it was not worth all the work. If it didn't rain, everything dried up. Yet that didn't keep my dad from planting a garden again the next year. He always thought the next year would be better. It was a different story with my mother. She had limited hearing and often counted on me to provide her the missing pieces of information she didn't hear. My filling this role for her was good for me. It made me positive, and it gave me the urge to try the impossible. I don't know the specific reasons for this quality, but I do know that I'm always positive. Sometimes I think I'm too positive, and it turns people off. I can't help that I am positive. I am what I am, and positive is what I am.

My favorite aunt felt it was time for me to learn to ride a bicycle. I was tall for my age, and she said I would have more fun if I could ride a bicycle. So she bought a bicycle and leaned it up against the side of the apartment building. That was a good place to have it, as it was a meeting place for all the kids on the block. I could hardly wait to sit on it. Well, that is exactly what I did; I sat on it. I was afraid to peddle it! A couple of days went by before everyone realized I couldn't ride a bicycle. So they decided to push me. Wow! They pushed me over the curb and back up on the sidewalk. Some kids ran in front, hollering at the people walking toward us to get out of the way. Then one of the kids hollered that they were going to give me a big shove, and I would be on my own. My aunt screamed from the upstairs window to hold tight onto the handlebars and peddle fast. All of a sudden, I was on my own peddling as fast as I could and loving it.

During the war my dad was offered a job cooking for the United States Army in the South. That small southern town seemed to have not one place to rent. My dad didn't know what to do, as he couldn't stay unless we had a place to live. He talked to the officer in charge. The officer talked to the mayor, and the mayor talked to the owners of a large plantation. The owners came and talked to my dad. They said they would have a place for us within a week in the very center of an orange grove. The house needed some cleaning up, and we were welcome to stay with them in the main house until ours was ready. I had so much fun when we lived with them. I had many children to play with all day. Every evening when the work was done everyone sat on the front porch and sang. Breakfast, lunch, and dinner were very formal with starched tablecloths, place settings, flowers, and ladies in white and black dresses serving. No one started eating until everyone was seated, bowed their heads and closed their eyes and said a prayer. I had to wear a dress, socks and shoes to the table. They took a lot of time teaching me proper table manners, things that were new to me. I liked these owners so well, and they were so nice with their southern accents, that I did everything they told me to do.

One day I was walking in the center of the railroad track with my girlfriend on our way home from school. We were taking our time, picking up chunks of coal, and seeing who could throw them the farthest. In one area, we had to balance and walk very carefully, as there was water below. We saw some kids in our class swimming; they told us to jump in. My girlfriend threw her shoes over onto the grass and jumped in right away. I said, "I can't. I don't know how to swim." Before I knew it, someone behind me had shoved me, and I was under the water just about ready to surface. Two of our friends swam up to my side and took my shoes off. They showed me how to dog paddle, and I caught on right away. I don't know why I wasn't scared, but I wasn't at all. I suppose it had all happened so fast. Someone ran and told my mother; she came running down to get me. I thought I was going to get in trouble because I was wet from head to toe in my nice, new school dress that she'd just made for me. She just stood there with her hands on her hips and a smirk on her face. She never said a word.

Jackie Gleason knew what he was talking about when he said, "How Great It Is!" It was great to have a positive dad, a supportive mother, a favorite aunt who wanted me to ride a bicycle, plantation owners who taught me good manners, and school friends who taught me how to dog paddle.

One and Only Family Reunion

Our one and only Lundgren Family Reunion took place at Rush Lake in Michigan. I was just fourteen at the time, but I had a driver's license and really felt I was special and important because I was the first one in my junior high school to have a Florida driver's license. My mother liked my having a license, as I could drive her to the many grocery stores that had special sales. We didn't save money, as we always had to put gas in the car that was fourteen cents a gallon, but we had a lot of fun. I felt great driving to stores and not having to take the trolley and carry the groceries home in those big brown sacks.

Then when my aunts visited, I could drive them everywhere. It was especially fun taking everyone to the Million Dollar Pier in St. Petersburg to go swimming. My aunts had funny-looking bathing suits. We lived in the South and we made ours, but they had the same bathing suit all of their lives, and not one of them fit. None of my aunts on either side of the family ever drove a car, and it was years before I finally figured it out that all of them were hard of hearing. They said that they didn't feel it was safe to drive when you didn't hear well.

All four of my aunts and my mother jabbered away in English and Swedish with a lot of "huh's" and "eh's," and so much laughter even though they didn't hear what each other was saying. They always huddled together and laughed and carried on for hours.

Aunts, uncles, and cousins by the dozens showed up for the reunion. It was an ordeal when it was time to go, just to decide who was going to ride with who, and to sort out all the confusion of getting us all in the cars. We didn't ride with the cousins we wanted to. I was in Uncle Clifford and Aunt Anna's car from Jamestown, New York. Neither one of them drove, but Uncle Clifford bought it because his brother and wife were coming to visit from Sweden, and that brother drove us to the family reunion. Aunt Minnie was in the front seat because she didn't want to drive her Cadillac up to Rush Lake, as the last two miles was a dirt road that led to Uncle Franz and Aunt Ruth's log cabin. I was jammed in the back seat between my two cousins that I didn't know well. I discovered later that they were really not my cousins, but related to the wife of our driver from Sweden. They kept elbowing me and laughing. Finally everyone was in the cars, and we formed a line and followed each other, starting from the front of Aunt Emma and Uncle Ed's house at 5907 Mead Avenue in Dearborn, Michigan, which was by the Fordson Elementary School near Michigan Avenue and Schaffer Road.

It was about a two-hour drive to get to Rush Lake. I kept wondering why everyone was passing and waving to us with big grins on their faces. I was tired of being so crushed sitting in the back seat, so I edged up and asked why we were not going faster and why was there so much noise. The driver muttered that the car would not go any faster and that it was not a very good car. When we stopped at the next light, he shifted into first gear and held down the clutch with his left foot. When the light finally turned to green, he jerked his foot little by little, gained very little speed, shifted into second gear, and went just a fraction faster. I kept waiting for him to shift into third gear, but it never happened, so I asked him what was the matter and why he didn't shift again. He didn't know what I was talking about and said there were no more gears, plus he told me to sit back on the seat till we got there. I couldn't shut up, and I kept telling everyone that there was another gear. I knew there was another gear. He said he knew the car well, as he had just driven it from Jamestown, New York to Dearborn, Michigan, all in second gear! I finally persisted enough not only to agitate everyone in the car, but also to agitate the driver enough that I convinced him to put his left foot down on the clutch again, and I would shift down into third gear, which I did. Finally, we were able to catch up with some of the others.

My mother would have been a nervous wreck in this car. I can just see her now, chewing her one-third stick of Beemans gum, folding the silver paper, and stuffing it in and out of the black and white wrapper.

Ours was the last car to arrive at the family reunion at Rush Lake. Uncle Helmer and Uncle Oscar, who had milk deliveries and left much later than we did and had to drive their cumbersome milk trucks in the late afternoon traffic, were already there jumping off the dock! They swam to the raft where ice cold drinks were in a sack hung in the water attached to the raft that waited for them.

Everyone wondered why the driver changed clothes when we arrived, hosed down the inside of the car, took off his shoes, and scraped and washed them off. It was because I told him I was feeling queasy, and he wouldn't listen to me. I had barfed all down his right side, hitting his right foot that he used for the brake. Everyone was gagging, but what could I do? I'd tried to tell him, and he wouldn't listen. No one wanted me to ride back with them. I wonder why?

When I Grow Up

Aunts, uncles, and cousins by the dozens, along with friends and classmates always ask me where I enjoyed living the most. Was it where I lived in the north or south or east or west? My answer has always been the same. I enjoyed everywhere I lived. It didn't make any difference whether it was north, south, east or west. It was always easy for me to make new friends in the schools. And I always made new friends where we lived. In the north, we lived in big apartment buildings. In the south, we lived in a small house. In the east, we lived in an apartment building that had a place to play on the premises, and in the west, we lived in a duplex, there were so many of them.

Dad and mom had sisters and brothers in the north and south. It was a lot of fun visiting them. Usually we saw them every three to four years, or less. I loved getting together with my cousins. Mealtime was always a special occasion with many laughs. They asked my dad if this is the way he would make the soup or stew or whatever was served. My dad always said the food was delicious, but you could add a little more of this or that. I was proud of my dad.

After dinner the women would go into the kitchen to clean up, and the men would go outside for a smoke. My cousins and I would see who could get out the door first. If you were first out the door, you chose what game we played. There was a lot of pushing and shoving going out the door. After an hour or so, we were called in to come to the table for dessert. Wow! What a selection of desserts! My favorites were chocolate cake and pudding. There wasn't any dessert I didn't like, but the chocolate cake and pudding were to die for. There was always plenty for everyone, and sometimes we could have two choices if we ate all our dinner. I don't remember anyone not eating all his or her dinner. Leaving after a couple of days was hard for me because I was having such a good time, but Dad was anxious to find work.

East and west seemed like they took so much more time to get to. Going from the east to the west, the scenery changed a lot. Each had its own beauty. Pueblo mud houses were so different from the chickees built in the south. The Pueblos built their houses up on high cliffs. We drove half way up a cliff where they sold baskets and aqua ornaments to wear. We visited the Seminole chickees in the Everglades and watched the mothers sit on the floor and make dolls to sell using their Singer sewing machines. I have one of those dolls made by Mary Osceola. In the east, we always bought maple syrup, and in the west and south we always benefitted from orange groves.

What a life, living in the north, south, east, and west! I enjoyed everywhere my dad got a job, traveling with my folks as my mom read from our one-volume encyclopedia, and I looked at my mother's face when she took a little snooze. Then I thought to myself, "Will I look so beautiful when I grow up?"

A Michigan lake

Winter Haven, Florida

CHAPTER 4

CONSTANTLY INQUISITIVE

Chicken in a Basket

From time to time, highway signs had words I recognized and could read to my folks as we traveled from one state to another when Dad was looking for a job. "Get your chicks on Route 66!" is what I remember seeing on the signs. The word was actually "kicks" but I'd turned it into "chicks". I was excited and had many questions such as, "Daddy, why would you put chicken in a basket? Don't these food places where we stop have plates?" My dad didn't know the answer, so it was a mystery to all three of us. I could hardly wait to stop somewhere to see how they put a chicken in a basket.

Mother said not to get too excited, that chicken is chicken no matter how you fix it. Then my dad decided it would be very messy eating chicken from the basket without a fork and knife, and he wondered if they would serve it with a fork and knife. He couldn't imagine cutting up a chicken to eat in a basket. Even when you hold it down with a fork, it squirms on a plate as you try to cut it. My mother thought they would serve it in small pieces and you wouldn't have to cut it up. I wanted to have only the white meat and wondered how I would manage to do that. My idea was to order only two chickens in the baskets and I could have the white meat, my mother would have the brown meat. My dad's favorite was always the wings and neck. He said he would cut the meat off the legs for Mom and I. We kept talking about this new experience we were going to have if we ever reached the restaurant. If the restaurant had a drive-in, I wanted us to pull up to the drive-in area, as I liked to see the carhops and wanted them to serve us. I just knew they could tell us all about this new way of serving chicken.

We finally got to the restaurant and they had a drive-in area where carhops served you. A very large sign in front of the restaurant said "Chicken in a Basket" with a picture of a funny-looking yellow chicken. We went inside to wash our hands. I was so excited to get back to the car, but I had to wait for my folks before I could order. They came out of the restaurant smiling. I wondered what they had learned, but they didn't say a word. The carhop came over in her cute uniform with a picture of a basket on her apron with a yellow chicken in the basket. My dad let me place the order for three chickens in a basket with two cups of coffee and a tall glass of milk. Before she left, she attached the tray to the window of our car door.

The carhop was back within ten minutes with our drinks and handed the three chicken baskets to us. The baskets were lined with red and white checked, waxy paper. They had a fried chicken cut up in sections so you didn't need a knife and a big pile of French fries with ketchup on the side. She gave each one of us three big, paper napkins. This was a treat that turned out to be a scrumptious feast. Every place where my dad worked, we could not stop talking about our "chicken in a basket" lunch.

Pansy Lady

I have always loved pansies! My mother started them from seeds and planted them in old tin cans. Together we drew pictures of our favorite flower and glued the pictures onto the cans. My mom even made the glue. We got the cans ready ahead of time so that when spring came, they were ready for planting. We saved them every year for this special occasion. Those old tin cans were rusty and full of holes, yet my dad never complained about carrying them around in the trunk of his car. They were ready for the seeds we'd plant come spring.

Many times we were on the road going to another town to find a job for Dad, but no matter where we were, when the first day of spring arrived, out came the tin cans. Dad and mom watched as I planted seeds in the cans. We chanted: "A pansy for you. A pansy for me. A pansy for Daddy who drives our pansies to our new place to live!" I gave them their drink of water every morning and evening. Mom didn't want me to flood them, so she limited the amount of water by having me suck on a straw to get the water out of my tin cup to water the seeds.

Mom had me count how many different colors of pansies I saw in yards in the town and in the country. Most of the time I saw orange, white, yellow, blue, purple, and red pansies in the front yards of homes. I really liked yellow ones because I always thought they were smiling at me. One time I called excitedly to my mom that there was a black pansy by the side of the station where my dad was having the gas station man fill our gas tank. He was very friendly and said that his wife planted pansies along the side of the ladies' restroom every year, and that the soil must be just right, as sometimes they bloomed both in the summer and in the fall. His wife saw us and walked over. She told me with a twinkle in her eye, as she winked at my mother, that the pansies smile at her and she talks to them. Just as we were ready to climb back into the car, she told me to wait a minute. She had something for me. She gave me one of her husband's blue cloths that he used for cleaning windows. It had twelve seeds for us to plant in our cans in the spring. She said that she would always remember me with my curly red hair, my smile, and my love for her favorite flower, the pansy. I waved to her till she was out of sight.

I don't even know her name, but when we planted those seeds, Mom and I called them Friendly Flowers from the Pansy Lady. And they were the best crop of pansies that ever grew in my tin cans.

Seminole Indians

It was always fun when we went around Lake Okeechobee because I knew we would see many Seminole Indians that lived in chickees in the Everglades. They were very friendly people. To get to their chickees, we walked over a bridge made of straw and wood, as the chickees were built on stilts in the water of cypress logs and palm thatch leaves woven together by vines and thin ropes. They had no walls, only thatched roofs that covered the area around the upward standing cypress logs. Some were two story chickees, but I never went in a two story one.

The men wore their slick black hair in a sort of bowl cut, and some wore a cloth turban. The women had a little bit of hair along their foreheads, long bangs, and a tight bun. They looked stunning with their rich shiny black hair. My dad and mom talked with the men who spoke a little English. Mom was interested in their basketry and their sewing. The ladies sat on the floor with their Singer hand-operated sewing machines, but there was no electricity. They were very fast in moving the round handle around and around. I sat with them and their children. We didn't speak much, but they touched my red curly hair after a while and laughed.

I liked their very colorful, floor-length dresses and long-sleeved blouses trimmed with ruffles. Each one wore a glass necklace. The older they got, the more beads their necklace had. I counted them in English, and they counted in their language. Their babies had a strand of beads at birth that was added to every year. When they were getting older, the grandmas stopped wearing so many strands of beads, as they became uncomfortable. The men wore plain shirts with built-in belts that were tucked into their trousers during the week. They had a long shirt with many ruffles for dress. All the material was cotton, and calicos were most common. I liked their stripes, solids, and plaids.

We stopped at their village every year when we went south. This time they were making cloth dolls. I didn't play with my one and only Shirley Temple doll, but I packed it in my suitcase, so it was always with me no matter where we lived. It was on a shelf in my clothes closet. But I really loved these dolls. They were cloth-wrapped palmetto fiber husk stuffed with cotton. The dolls' hairstyle looked very much like the Seminole women. I wanted one so badly. My folks didn't give in right away and teased me by saying that maybe on the way back we would buy one.

Before we left, dad bought some of their fry bread, which I liked, and their drink made out of grits or roasted corn. One of the men walked us back over the wobbly bridge to our car, and just as I was getting in the car he gave me a very colorful Seminole doll that I still have today. I was so happy. All the ladies smiled, waved, and shouted as I waved to them holding my doll when we drove away.

Sheeny Man

The Sheeny Man is a derogatory name for Jews who were peddlers or street vendors of junk. They were also called Ragmen. "If you don't behave, we'll sell you to the Sheeny Man." That was a very common threat children heard from mothers when they misbehaved. Sheeny Man was a man who rode the alley on a horse-driven cart, like a buckboard, and he collected things people threw away. These junkmen sold what they collected. Some of the Sheeny Men had hand-drawn carts and walked the streets. They bought and sold anything, fruit, linens, rags, junk, and old furniture. They were also called rag-and-bone men. Some of them became door-to-door salesmen and were the first recyclers, and the first to offer goods for sale on credit. They were immigrants, and this work helped them to support their families. It helped them to establish roots in our country. Outside of their immigrant communities, the rag-and-bone men were shunned as scavengers and beggars. Their work was considered humiliating. I remember seeing posters, "No Beggars or Peddlers Allowed." They were equated to the bogeyman so that children who heard threats that they'd be sold to the Sheeny Man were quite afraid and tended to improve their behaviors.

As a child living in Detroit on the fourteenth floor of a brick apartment building, I loved it when the Sheeny Man came around. The first thing we heard was the clinking and clattering of pots and pans. I ran down all the flights of stairs and children from every floor did the same. We all ran down as fast as we could go. Some of the older kids skipped two or three steps at a time, but I couldn't skip steps. I had to take one at a time. I wasn't the first out the door, but I always managed to catch up with the others. We all followed the Sheeny Man, hanging on to the side of his cart and swatting everything within reach that made a noise. A couple of the bigger boys climbed up onto the buckboard with the Sheeny Man. I never did that because it was too high up.

When the Sheeny Man stopped to make a sale, he took the time to show us many nice items that he had for sale, so we would tell our folks when we went home. After about an hour, he drove back closer to where we lived and pointed the way for all of us to walk back home. He told us all to walk together and not to go into another neighborhood. He watched us until we were out of sight. We turned around and waved and hollered to him. He was always friendly and nice.

Sometimes we brought him a cookie. He always told us how good it was, and he ate the cookie very slowly so it would last longer. The Sheeny Man was called many names that were not so nice, but my dad would not allow my friends or me to be disrespectful. Dad always said that the man was a hard-working man, making an honest living so he could support his family. I really loved the Sheeny Man.

Nice Mrs. Sorbinski

"Mom, why am I different? Is it because I have red hair? I saw a girl in another grade at school, and she had red hair."

"No, it's not because you have red hair. Many people of all ages have red hair."

"Is it because I was born with a red birthmark on my leg?"

"No, it's not because you have a red birthmark on your leg. Lots of people have a birthmark on their bodies."

"You tell me sometimes that I am different? Why do you think that? Is it bad to be different?"

"No, it's not bad to be different. I'm so glad that you are different. I think you are different because you ask lots of questions. You notice many things that other children do not. You are happy every morning when you wake up. You enjoy going to school every day and Sunday school every Sunday. You invite all your friends to go to the park and never leave anyone out. You are never bored. You can always think of something to do. You never say that there is nothing to do. You know how to play without any toys or your friends. I could make a list longer than a sheet of your school notebook paper. "

"Mrs. Sorbinski told me the other day that I was different. She said that is why she liked me so much. She looked at Rosie and Tony and said to them that they should be more like me and get outside and play instead of whining and moping around the house saying there was nothing to do and no one to play with today. She told them to always look for me, and I would start something fun with them."

"That was nice of Mrs. Sorbinski. She's a nice lady. She's so busy cooking for her family of nine. Her husband works long hours at the factory. He leaves early in the morning and comes home late at night. This Sunday why don't you invite Rosie and Toni to go to Sunday school with you? Tell her I will walk all of you there, and I'll be right there to walk you home."

"Ok. I'll run over and ask her right now. I think Rosie and Toni will want to go, as they like the Bible stories that I tell them when I get home from Sunday school."

The following Sunday morning Rosie and Tony were at our back door 20 minutes early, ready to go with my mom and me to Sunday school. Mom walked with us and was right outside when we came out. They were so happy, and we showed mom the picture that we colored with these words by C. Herbert Woolston, 1856-1927.

Jesus loves the little children, all the children of the world.
Red and yellow, black and white, they are precious in His
sight. Jesus loves the little children of the world.

"Isn't it wonderful that each one of you colored the same picture, and each picture is beautiful and different? God loves variety. That's why He made each one of you different. We all jumped up and down, and all of us held hands walking and skipping back home singing *Jesus Loves the Little Children.*

Washing Machines

Do you know anyone who doesn't have a washing machine? I don't. It's easy to go to one of the big chain stores and buy a washing machine today. They advertise no down payment, and you don't make your first payment for six months. Wow! Is this a deal, or isn't it?

In this day and age, whether you have the money or not, you buy what you want most of the time. Not necessarily what you need. Credit is made easy. The shock comes when you finally wake up later and realize how much interest you are paying. If you lose your job, you still get notices to make your payment. The notices keep coming. If you miss half a dozen payments, you begin to get notices from a collection agency, and you are in more debt. Then you begin to wonder, was the washing machine really worth it? Then you ask yourself, why, oh why, did I fall for this in the first place? It would be a relief not to have to make all the monthly payments.

A laundromat is only ten minutes from the house, and a chat with some of the people in the laundromat would be fun. Sometimes you could read a book or magazine while waiting. My grandmother never had a washing machine. She had a big scrub board she used for really dirty clothes Grandpa wore to work in the coalmine. Grandmother boiled a large tub of water on the stove, the same tub we all took baths in on Saturday night. She stirred the dirty clothes back and forth, up and down with a wooden stick. After she did this several times, she pulled up the clothes with the stick and set them down in a big pan on the floor. While the next batch of clothes was being boiled, she carried the washed clothes outside. This took several trips. When we were there, one of us pumped water over them, and Grandmother wrung them out by hand. If any of the men were home, they helped wring them out too. She then hung them up on the clothesline. It was strung from tree to tree outside the back door, not far from the pump. This whole process was done every Monday, and it took all day.

My great grandma told us about how she pounded the clothes on rocks in the river, or rubbed them with grainy sand. I saw all the local people in Africa where I lived washing their clothes like this in the rivers, while their children splashed, jumped around, and played.

The first washing machine I remember seeing was made of wood. A handle that helped tumble the clothes stuck out the side. You put your clothes one at a time through two small rollers. The next washing machine I remember was fun. It squashed the clothes dry with a hand-operated wringer built onto the top of the machine. After that, my mother took the clothes out to the washing line and hung them up. This machine was replaced by an electric-powered washing machine. It was a drum-type with a galvanized tub and an electric motor. Maytag deserves a compliment. He first started with a wooden tub. Eventually he surfaced with the electric motor-driven wringer washing machine.

The day these machines arrived, all the women in the apartment building were thrilled and excited. They had to take turns by signing up to use them. Housewives had a way of seeing who got what first. When one of the ladies in the neighborhood invited everyone over for coffee and "whoopee do - guess what?" she had everyone walk down the stairs to the basement, and she proudly showed off her new Whirlpool washing machine. Many "oohs" and "aahs" followed. "It's amazing," one of the ladies said, "that we have gone from boiling our clothes to hand wringers, electric ringers, and now we have the Whirlpool!"

Today, households have two separate machines. One is an automatic washing machine that washes, rinses, and spins clothes dry. The other machine is the dryer where clothes are thrown straight from the washing machine in order to be tumbled dry. Gone is the all-day chore you of washing and hanging clothes to dry. That chore has been replaced with "automatic" machines.

One person said washing machines and marriages are similar. They have much in common. They both click on from cycle to cycle. They get in a spin from time to time. Best of all, they both make things all right again and come out with a clean slate when it is all over. They do the job and they do it right.

I'm fortunate. I don't do the wash either by hand or by machine! I lived with my parents until I graduated from college, and my mother always did the wash. My aunt took care of my clothes when I moved to another state to accept my first teaching position. I've been married many years, and my husband took over the wash before we were married until this day. I don't think I want to even consider buying the latest washing machine. I'm perfectly happy to have others wash my clothes in any machine they choose. I'm blessed beyond words.

Here Comes the Ice Truck

It was a fun time when the iceman drove up in his truck to carry ice up all the flights of stairs in our apartment building three times a week. No one had electric refrigerators, but everyone had an icebox. Ours was made out of wood, and the block of ice sat in the bottom. If you wanted ice delivered, you placed your sign in the window, and the iceman cut a block of ice for the family.

The iceman's job was really hard, and he worked from daylight to sundown. He wore a leather sling and a shoulder pad to help him carry the ice on his shoulder. I watched him cut the ice block to just the right size with his tongs and ice pick. He knew the size each family wanted. Doors were never locked, and he didn't knock, but just walked right on in. If no one was home, cash was left on the table for him. He whistled when he came flying down the steps to get his next block of ice to carry up the steps.

Along with the other kids on the block, I watched him walk out of sight for the next delivery. Then we scrambled to get up in the back of the truck and pick at the slivers of ice between the grooves of the wood floor. When he came back, he hollered at us and pretended he was mad. We hid under his truck and in the nearby alley till he was out of sight again, and then jumped back up onto the truck to pick up the slivers of ice to suck on. I actually think he scraped extra ice off just for us.

Sometimes when we were out of ice, our moms gave us a dime and several of us trampled with one of the kids' wagon down to the Ice House. An older man sat on a stool in front of the Ice House with his tongs and ice pick. He sold us some ice. We showed him our money, and he went in and cut a block of ice for us. He was really nice, but didn't talk much. While taking the ice home, we picked up objects from the curb and placed them on the ice to make a design. The ice melted some going home, so we had to hurry and not play around too much. Sometimes we took turns sitting on the ice blocks; it felt cool and soothing.

Getting the ice up the flights of stairs to the 14th floor was a challenge. I went around and knocked on doors; always someone came to the rescue. One man who helped me worked night shift, so he got out of bed and carried the ice up. Mom gave him a cup of coffee with a sweet bread crust. He always smiled, but hurried downstairs to go back to bed before he had to go to work.

A real treat for me was when my mother wrapped a small chunk of ice in a towel for me to suck on to cool me off before I went to bed. I really looked forward to this time with my mother as we sat by the window. She sang to me or read poems from our one-volume encyclopedia.

Milk in Glass Bottles

Milk sold in glass bottles was convenient for people and more sanitary. Sometimes we bought it in the local neighborhood store. Many times we took our bucket or pails that we saved only for milk to the farm. It was more fun going to the farm, but our car was not always available, as Dad used it to drive to work. My mother didn't usually go to the farm due to there not being enough room in the neighbor's car, but I squeezed in and went with the family that went to the farm.

Going to the farm was a fun time because the mothers visited, and all of us kids ran all over the farm. We jumped from row to row in the gardens, pulled the pails up and down at the well and washed our hands and faces, ran through the barns from one end to the other, and best of all, watched the women and men milking the cows. They always warned us to stay back. If cows got nervous, they would kick us. We got our buckets and pails filled while they were milking the cows, and we took them over to set beside the car.

Sometimes we were invited in to the farmhouse for cold milk. The adults had coffee with what they called pure cream. I didn't like pure cream at all, but everyone else raved over it. Loaves of freshly baked bread with homemade butter to spread on it were ever so good.

It was quite a miracle to hold the buckets and pails of milk on the ride home and not to spill any in the car. We had covers to hold over them, but they didn't fit tightly. When we got home and took the milk to the apartments, everything had to come out of the icebox to fit the milk in. In the winter when it was cold, milk was stored on the porch in a homemade wooden box.

My mother liked it when the milkman delivered bottles right to our door. Some of the bottles had stoppers on wire loops, designs embossed on the glass, and hard wax to cover the milk. We had a small metal box that sat on the front doorstep. Milk, eggs, butter, and sometimes orange juice were delivered to that box. We rinsed out the used bottles and left them in the box to be picked up at the next delivery time. Mom wrote a note and left it in the metal box if she wanted something. My aunt who lived in a house had a little space in the wall by her side door. The milkman left the deliveries, and she got them through a small door on the inside without having to go outside into the weather.

When my apartment friends and I saw the milkman arrive, we followed him to every house and helped him deliver milk bottles and other items on the neighbors' lists. We had a nice milkman everywhere we lived, and we had so much fun going around with him. My favorite milkman was my mother's brother. He always had a smile and joked around with us.

Hanging Out the Window

All I could think of when we lived in the small town near Plant City, Florida was how annoyed I was to be there. It was hot and sticky! I had not wanted to leave Dearborn, Michigan where I was close to my aunts, uncles, cousins, and friends in their neighborhoods. It was fun to interact with so many children my own age that spoke not only English, but also the language of their parents who'd come over from their country of birth, "the old country".

My dad didn't have a job, so we had driven to Florida where it was warm before the first snowfall to enroll me in school, which was a first for me. I wasn't sure whether I'd like school or not. I really enjoyed my mother reading to me from our one-volume encyclopedia and writing letters of the alphabet on the back of receipts. I traced carefully over all the letters.

I grumbled and made it known that I didn't like hot, sticky weather, mosquitoes, sand spurs or drops of perspiration on my nose. They responded by telling me how much fun it was going to be swimming in the lakes, Gulf of Mexico, and even the ocean year round, as the water never got cold enough to freeze and make ice. Schools in Florida got out by noon, so I'd have more time to play.

I was not the best passenger on our trip to Florida, as I got carsick on the long, narrow, windy, and sometimes sandy roads. We always stopped for breakfast, lunch and dinner. Late afternoons we looked for a sign in the windows of homes in the small towns advertising where we could stay overnight.

That was fun. Sometimes I was even able to play with children where we stayed until it was time to go to bed. The people provided breakfast for us in the morning when we surfaced, and then we were on the road again. It took four to five days to get to Florida. We drove in and out of two or three cities before Dad found a job. As soon as my dad got a job, we found a place to live, and he took me to school the very next morning before he went to work. My mother picked me up and we walked home by way of a park, the nearest swimming hole, or the beach.

I attended many schools and enjoyed every one. Even though I don't remember all their names, I remember two especially well. One was a small two-story school in Winter Haven, Florida and the other was the school in the Big Bayou. The teacher in the school near Plant City wore slippers because of her age and encouraged me to listen carefully to the story she read, so I could answer questions at the end of the story. Then I could go out to play. It was so hot in the room that I went over to the window. She asked me to sit down, but I was so uncomfortable and didn't want to be in class that I climbed up on the window, jumped out, and held on to the windowsill. I told her I would come in if she would let me go home. She promised she would, and I climbed back into the classroom. She kept her word and walked me home while the principal sat in the room with the class. My mother was petrified and made me promise I would not do that again. In a couple of weeks, we moved from that area and I didn't have to go to school until I entered first grade.

I really enjoyed Lakewood Elementary in the area of Big Bayou in St. Petersburg, Florida. We were there for six months in sixth grade. I loved it. On the way home every day I went swimming with some of the kids in my class. The teacher took a great interest in me and gave me two to three books a week to read at home. She really set the stage for my life-long love of reading. My mother also read every book that I brought home and we discussed them. The teacher gave me a list of thirty-two books to read in the summer, so that I would be ready for junior high school in September.

Another school I remember well was in Cleveland, Ohio. On a winter day walking to school, or I should say running the two miles to school as it was so cold, I was knocked down by two kids from the back, two from the front and a tripper from the side. It was a shock and it knocked the breath out of me, but soon I caught my breath and slowly got up. I was a little late to school, but my teacher understood.

When I look back on the many schools I attended, I realize that all the teachers were kind to me, and they loved and encouraged me during my years in elementary school. I realize I have been blessed.

Brown and White Bicycle

My heart's desire was to have a bicycle of my very own. It wasn't because I knew how to ride a bicycle because I didn't. But I pretended by sitting on the seat of someone else's bike with my feet on the pedals, leaning against the wall of an apartment building or a tree. My dad had a black sedan, so when we moved, we could bring my bicycle, if I ever had one. At that time, all bikes seemed to be red or blue, and occasionally green. None of those colors appealed to me at all. I wanted a different color.

After Dad came home for work at night, we three always took a walk. Mom and I looked forward to it. Dad never complained even though he'd been on his feet all day, from 4:00 am to 8:00 pm. He must have really been tired. As he left work, he always told the crew that he was taking his favorite ladies for a walk. As we walked, we window-shopped. One night we walked farther than usual. Stores were decorating their windows for Christmas, still two months away. We finally reached the big Sears, Roebuck and Co. store. Mom and I liked this store because it had such big window displays. One of the windows had the most beautiful bike I had ever seen in my life. It was a girl's brown and white bicycle with a front basket and tires with white sidewalls. I was in awe! I couldn't believe my eyes! I jumped up and down and shouted with glee. After that, every night we had to walk past the Sears, Roebuck and Co. store to look at that bicycle. I was praying and hoping no one would buy it.

I told everyone about that bicycle. No one shared my enthusiasm. My aunts and uncles were polite and nice, but my friends, classmates, and cousins could care less. They said, "Why do you like brown and white, when everyone has red, blue or green? I think you just like being different. Brown and white is not good looking." I tried to defend myself, but it was useless. And I knew we could never afford a new bike for me, but I still wanted to walk way out of our way to see it every night. Secretly, I was hoping for a miracle. My folks would tease me a little bit, and explain that you can't always have what you want, even though they'd love to buy it for me. I told them I understood, but I really wanted that bike to replace riding the busses and trolleys to the beaches. Most of my friends had a bike by 5th grade, but we were always moving. I'd never wanted a bike that much, before this brown and white one caught my attention.

One night when we went to look at the bike, it was gone. My dream of owning and riding that bike was shattered. I felt so bad. My Swedish Sunday school teacher comforted me, and she prayed that the girl who got that bike would be a blessing to others. She also prayed that the Lord would give me a bike someday that I could love as much as this brown and white one.

Christmas morning came. We always got up at 3:30 am as dad had to get to work to turn on all the ovens. Christmas was the busiest day of the year at the restaurant. I sleepily got out of bed and walked into the front room. The three of us sat on the sofa, the Christmas tree lights went on, and there in front of the tree was the brown and white girl's bike! I jumped for joy! The three of us hugged and kissed each other. Dad went to work, and Mom put the turkey in the oven. I took my bike outside, and with my mom's help pushing me down the dirt road, I learned to ride the most beautiful brown and white bike in the world.

Kool-Aid with Powdered Sugar

"Hooray! It's the last day of school! We get out early! Now we can drink Kool-Aid every day!" one of the boys hollered as he took his one and only packet of cherry-flavored Kool-Aid out of his back pocket.

Kool-Aid came in many flavors, but the favorites were cherry, raspberry, orange, and strawberry. No one had powdered sugar with them, but we all agreed to meet at the park close to the end of the trolley line, and one would bring a bucket and stick to mix it, and one would bring a box of powdered sugar. We all took turns bringing the Kool-Aid and the sugar. We all had our plastic glasses. They looked awful after a while. We rinsed our glasses in the fountain at the park. We were going to hide our glasses in a tree, but my mother said we could store them on the orange crate box we used as a table at our house on our front-screened porch.

The end of the first week of summer we had a contest to see who could drink the most glasses of Kool-Aid in five minutes. Twenty-some glasses full of strawberry Kool-Aid were lined up in a row on the cement table in the park by the fountain. Five fellas and four girls decided to be in the contest. The winner got to go to the movie free the following Saturday. We all chipped in and bought the movie ticket. Only one of us had a watch and that was Isabella. She put her hand up when it was one minute and everyone hollered "One minute!" This was how it went for every minute till she held up her hand, and everyone hollered, "Five minutes!" The contestants stopped drinking. Only three lasted the five minutes. Two fellas and one girl made it. They not only looked bad, they were sick. Those who dropped out before the five minutes were up were leaning over the wall of the fountain barfing. The last three joined them before long. Tony drank the most glasses, and he won the free movie ticket. He didn't feel good either.

I didn't join in with them because I didn't like Kool-Aid in any flavor. There was a root beer flavored Kool-Aid, but I only liked the real root beer in a bottle. None of those friends ever sipped or licked the powder of Kool-Aid the rest of that summer. Till this day I do not like Kool-Aid with powdered sugar.

Sometimes we collected old newspapers and laid them down on the sidewalk. Then we used our worn-out toothbrushes and used Kool-Aid as paint. We mixed a little dirt with it to make it thicker. It worked fairly well, but ants and other little creatures soon discovered our art and quickly nothing was left of our Kool-Aid masterpieces.

Summer was a time to explore and have lots of fun with my fun friends.

Feast of the Fireflies

It was a hot summer night. My mother gave me a jar and out the door I went to catch as many fireflies that would fit in my jar. Sometimes I caught seven or eight at a time. Every time one escaped from the jar, I just continued to catch more till the jar was full. It was fun seeing them light up at night and even light up in my jar. When the jar was full, I took it in the house and put it on my little desk in the bedroom. I watched the fireflies light up till I fell asleep. When I woke up in the morning, I let them go. My mother and I made up songs about the fireflies. My Sunday school teacher taught me *Fireflies in Flight*. She had learned it from her mother. We sang it to the tune of *Camptown Races*.

"Fireflies in Flight" (author unknown)
Fireflies come out at night.
Blink, blink, blink, blink.
Showing off their little lights
In the summer sky!

Can you see them glow
Flying to and fro?
Fireflies come out at night
In the summer sky!

One of the mothers decided to get all the children in the neighborhood to have a contest to see who caught the most fireflies. The prize would be one of her homemade cherry pies. We all loved her pies. So that evening when it finally got dark enough to see the fireflies, we all lined up in front of our houses. She hollered out, "One, two, three. GO!" Off we scrambled to catch fireflies. It was no problem catching them as there were so many, but I was not fast enough to win. You had to catch them with your hand, carefully put them in your jar, and cover your jar so they wouldn't fly out. Everyone was whooping and hollering and having lots of fun. A fella we called Red was the first one to get his jar filled to the top. He not only had his jar full, he had some in his hand.

Out came the mother with three big cherry pies, and all of us had a big slice of pie along with some ice cream that two of the mothers added to our feast. We called this the Feast of the Fireflies. As we were gorging our pie and ice cream, we all decided to meet at the corner of the block in the morning to let all our fireflies out of our jars at the same time. Off we went to bed with our tummies full. We looked at our fireflies from our beds, thinking they were blinking at us and happy to know they would have their freedom first thing in the morning with all the other fireflies. We knew how to play and have fun just by catching fireflies!

Hula Hoop Time

Hula hoops were not very expensive, so almost everyone could buy one. They came in all colors. Every evening I watched out my bedroom window to see kids hula hooping between the two apartment buildings. I lived on the fourteen floor, so I had a great view. Kids hung out the windows on all the floors to watch. It was fun to holler to our friends, but after a while some parents got annoyed and told us to "knock it off," sometimes inserting a few "bad" words.

Hula hooping started right after dinner around 5:00 or 5:30 in the evening as dads came home from work. All the floors smelled good from food from many different countries cooking. It was best to get down between the buildings early, as it was first-come, first-serve. Hula hoopers ate as fast as they could and dashed out to get a good spot to start hooping right away. Some kids only lasted thirty minutes or so and stopped to sit off to the side, while other kids lasted for hours and only stopped when their parents called them to come in. They never wanted to stop, but calls from parents meant they stopped.

When kids first learned how to hula hoop, they started hooping around their waists. As they got better, they managed to hoop around their ankles and necks. Sometime they used two hula hoops at one time. Everyone on all the floors cheered them on. Saturday mornings, hula hoopers tried to help newcomers who didn't know how to swing. They lined up everyone by size, not by age, and started with the shortest. Little kids were funny to watch, but when they caught on, they could really swing, and they got their small hula hoops moving fast. The ones who didn't have good coordination kept on trying. All of them eventually could hula hoop.

I was tall for my age, so I was either in the next-to-the-oldest group or in the oldest group. I had a hard time catching on to the swinging, and my coordination was not good. I was well liked, so they took a lot of time to teach me. Everyone shouted for me to swing more. They told me not to look down at the hula hoop. I swung the hula hoop for about 8 minutes and down it went. Everyone still cheered! But I never was good enough to get on the team. I always went to all the competitions, and our apartment building walked away with many awards. Hula hooping was a lot of fun. Parents came out to watch us practice and perform. Evenings ended with lots of laughter and encouragement. Best of all, moms served cookies, popcorn, and lemonade!

At school, in one of the games at recess, we took turns spinning around till we got so dizzy we fell down. Our classmates helped get us back up and leaned us against the building. It was funny seeing lots of kids leaning against the building at the same time. Through all these inexpensive fun games I learned that we didn't have to go out and buy a game. We could make a game out of rock, clotheslines, old rubber tires, sticks, chalk, or hunks of black coal. In those days we made up our own games and everybody was included. That was true support. We were all one family.

One-Room Schoolhouse

I went to a one-room schoolhouse near the coal mines where my grandparents lived in Pennsylvania. I really enjoyed walking to school every day with the kids in the small mining town. That year the snow really came down thick and heavy! The older boys cleared a path so we could walk to school. It was always very cold walking even though everyone wore heavy coats, long underwear, leggings with boots, scarves, pull-down yarn hats, and mittens or gloves. Before we entered the school, the older boys brushed the snow off our clothes with straw brooms. When we got inside, we helped each other take off our boots. It was so nice to be inside, as the big, black stove was roaring out the heat from where it sat in the center of the room. The desks surrounded the stove. Older boys took turns getting there early to start the fire. Boots were lined up on the floor in the back according to size, and we were lined up according to how tall we were for our seat assignment. Everyone brought a tin lunch bucket that we kept under our desk.

When everyone was seated, the teacher had us stand up and say *The Pledge of Allegiance to the American Flag*, sing *God Bless America*, bow our heads as a prayer was said, and then sit down. We took turns reading something of our choice from the Bible. Our first subject of the day was reading. We took turns reading out loud and one of the 7th graders corrected us if we made a mistake. We had to pay close attention as each person read because the accents of four or five nationalities made it a challenge to understand. Everyone had the same book, and I enjoyed hearing Franco from Italy, Ingrid from Sweden, Charles from England, and Sophia from Germany. After our reading class was over, we stood and did a few exercises that included clapping our hands. Then we had a bathroom break. We took turns and went two-by-two; it was a two-holer. Because the snow was so deep and it kept snowing, we had a rope from the door of the classroom to the outhouse. We did not play around because it was so cold. We did what we had to do, held tight onto the rope, and got back to the classroom as quickly as our feet could take us. We wrote, colored, or played tic-tac-toe on the blackboard as we waited for everyone to get back. I always wanted to write a letter to my grandma or to a favorite aunt and uncle.

Writing was next and we first told the class what we wanted to write about, but before we wrote it we had to practice writing circles and up-and-down lines. Some of the older students helped the younger ones using the sample the teacher had on the blackboard. When the time was over, we stood and read what we wrote. The teacher chose the first one, and when that person finished, they chose the next person till everyone had a chance to read.

Arithmetic was the best. All of us wrote our problems on the black board that went from one wall to the other. We used rags to wipe off our mistakes. The teacher walked back and forth looking at all our work to make sure we didn't copy the person next to us. We told how we got the right answer, but if she suspected that we'd copied from the person beside us, she erased our work and watched us do the problem all over again.

My parents were concerned that I wouldn't be up to my class level when we went back to live in the city. I was in the beginning of algebra in the 4th grade, and when I enrolled in the 5th grade the next year in the city, the class was still in multiplication. I was well prepared in reading, writing, and arithmetic. I won the spelling bee, was chosen Student Teacher in reading, and my writing of one-page essays were on display every term. I loved my teacher and the classmates in the one-room schoolhouse. I was so fortunate to attend school in the coal mining town of Pennsylvania. Attending schools in many towns and many states through the years provided education beyond books that formed me into the person I am today. My parents were wise to provide that for me.

Coolator in the Passenger Window

My mom, dad and I were driving from the East coast to California during WWII, as my dad had a job as a chef in a VA hospital. The three of us were quite excited about the job Dad was offered. It was an opportunity to live in California.

"How far is California from Michigan, Dad?"

"I don't know, Joanie, but I think it's close to three thousand miles."

"How many miles have we gone so far, Dad?"

"Let's see. It looks like about 150 miles so far."

We got a late start, as we had to stop and get a green gas coupon book, so we could buy the gas we needed for this trip. We didn't get very far the first day. We were outside Minneapolis, driving up and down the streets of a nice neighborhood, looking for a sign on the lawn that read "Rooms For Rent". After what seemed like hours, we finally saw one and Dad got right out and knocked on the front screen door. A friendly lady came to the door, walked out to our car, took a good look at Mom and me, and said, "Welcome. Come right on in. I'll show you the bedroom and the bathroom. I have a pot of coffee on the stove, some cookies and milk." It was a nice big, comfy-looking bed with a striped, green cover on it. Next to the window was a cot for me with a pretty quilt she told us she had made especially for nice little girls. I loved it. I wanted to take it with me when we left, but it was not for sale. I fell asleep the minute I shut my eyes.

The next thing I knew my mom said we needed to hurry, as we were having a pancake breakfast. We ate the pancakes with real maple syrup and said our "goodbyes". We were on the road again.

It was getting really hot in the car even with all our windows open. We stopped for lunch in a small diner. My mom and I were slow in eating. Dad excused himself, walked to a local garage, and came back with a funny looking object. He said it was a coolator, and it would make the air in the car a lot more comfortable for us.

Some people call the coolator an old time icebox. It was a metal box that fit in the window of the passenger side of the car. You poured water into it and as you drove, it blew some cool air out. Even though it was very noisy, it really helped conquer the discomfort of being so hot.

A couple of days passed and the military stopped us occasionally to check if we were Americans. They asked each one of us our names, where we were born, where we were going, and what we were going to do in California. The last day we were about fifty miles from Needles, California. We were hungry and stopped. Dad fried eggs on the fender of the car, and we had bananas Mom sliced and put on white bread with peanut butter. We stopped at the border between Arizona and California. No fruit was allowed over the California line, so Dad gave it to the soldiers. We went directly to the VA office and Dad was assigned his job to start the following morning. We were told where we could rent a small apartment close by.

We liked the apartment, my new school, the people we met, and Dad liked his job. The adjustment to this new place was easy, and we three were very happy living in California.

WWII Victory Gardens

During WWII my dad, mom, and I lived in Dearborn, Michigan for a short period of time. It was Henry Ford's town and it was such a fun place to live. It was the only time I remember that my Dad didn't have a job as a chef. He was asked to work at the Vinco Tool and Die Company in Detroit that the brother-in-law of my Uncle Ed owned. My dad accepted the challenge. My dad and my uncle car-pooled to save gas, which was a very patriotic thing to do. They had extra gas stamps to buy gas on the weekends to take all of us for a drive to a park to have a picnic and to swim in the lake.

My mother didn't work, so she could help me plant a victory garden on the acreage by the school. It was a requirement that all students have a victory garden, and the gardens were inspected weekly, and we were given a grade. Grades were given in three colors: red, yellow, and green. Green was the passing grade. Yellow was not good enough, and red was bad. You had to have green, or you did not advance to the next grade. Students took this assignment seriously, as did their parents. I don't remember that anyone was held back. It was a fun time when parents helped their children in the victory garden every night after work. Everyone felt they were doing their patriotic duty. The Henry Ford family owned the land for the victory garden.

This was a new experience for me, not only to till the soil, but also to plant the seeds, water daily, and pull the weeds. I never saw so many weeds before in my life. It was a thrill for me to see my seeds grow. My mother and I did not miss a day walking down to our garden plot. The mothers talked to each other and laughed. All my classmates teased, laughed, ran up and down the rows, and actually measured their plants with rulers to see if theirs were the tallest. Rulers were given to all students at the elementary school every year from the local hardware store in the area. Walking home from the victory garden was fun because the sun was going down and we were all sweaty, dirty, and tired. A sad side to walking home was sometimes noticing a sign in the window of a home when a son or daughter was killed in action. Then everyone stopped for a moment of silence, and the Catholics made the sign of the cross. Occasionally, some of the dads who came home in time from work joined us, and we sang patriotic songs, stopped at the sidewalk in front of the homes where a family lived, waved "goodnight" with hugs and patted each other on the shoulder. I didn't get to see everyone walk up the sidewalk to their homes because I lived around the twelfth stop, and there were about twenty-five more houses to go.

We were a nice group of students working in the garden. When we finished our plot we went help kids who were having difficulties. The end of every week, red, green, and yellow flags were placed at our garden plots. We could hardly wait to see them. Everyone pitched in and helped the ones who were not doing well. Harvest time was a big event with neighbors and relatives galore anxious to see our produce and the flag. Following the ceremony everyone went to Lundgren's, my Uncle Franz and Aunt Ruth's ice cream store nearby, for a free ice cream cone.

"Hey Johnny, how come your tomatoes are bigger than all of ours?"

"I prayed for them."

"What? Are you crazy or something?"

"It worked, didn't it?"

"Yeah, I guess it did."

Where's Mom?

I don't know how many times I have walked in the back door of my folk's house and not seen my mom. I would frantically holler out, "Where's mom?" I raced from room to room, from the front of the house to the back, and then saw her hanging up clothes on the clothes line or picking fruit off the trees to make jelly or jam, or giving our Toy Manchester dog a bath.

I don't know why I felt panic. I was so anxious to see her because we would sit down, talk, and have a scone and a glass of milk or fresh orange juice from our orange tree. Once in a while we had a fresh loaf of bread out of the oven, still warm enough to melt the butter. If it wasn't too hot, my mom had a small table out in the backyard set with a pretty tablecloth with a small vase of hibiscus from our bushes that had red or orange flowers on them. I liked my mom's homemade guava jelly on my scone. Our guava fruit had pink flesh, but the house next door had yellow creamy flesh. They were soft and delicious. We took turns pulling the stem out of the center of the hibiscus flower to suck on it. It was a sweet taste. Sometimes when a neighbor joined us, Mom served her hibiscus tea.

After we talked for a long time, we took our dog, TOY, for a walk. He really didn't like to have a bath, so he stood under the table and was not friendly when we were munching away on my after-school snack, but when we rattled his dog leash that had tiny bells on it, he jumped for joy, as he knew we would walk him all around the city park. That took about an hour. It was a lovely park with winding sidewalks enhanced by many tropical plants, beautiful state palm trees, and manicured lawns.

Back at the house, and I changed out of my school clothes and went swimming for an hour with the neighbor children. It was a 20-minute walk from our house. The mothers took turns going with us. When I got back home and waved good-bye to my friends, for some reason I opened the back screen door and called out, "Where's Mom?" Mom always answered, "Here I am, Joanie. Let's listen to some music before we have dinner." She played the very first record I bought on my own, a Beethoven selection. I changed out of my wet bathing suit, hung it over the bathtub to dry, put on my pajamas, and sat beside my mom on the sofa. I felt so loved and comfy. I didn't have to say, "Where's mom?" She was right beside me.

Mother Always Outside Church

It was a very cold, snowy day and the sun was not in the sky, yet it was shining down on my mother and me. We walked slowly, holding hands, so as not to slip on the icy sidewalk and to stay close together to keep warm. It seemed a long way to the church, but it was only about twenty minutes from our apartment.

"Mom, why don't you go inside with me today as it is really cold? It's so nice and warm in there every Sunday. In my Sunday school classroom I can hear the radiators crackling."

"If my hearing was good I would go with you, Joanie. It's very frustrating and embarrassing for me when I can't hear the person speaking to me, and I have to ask them to repeat what they just said."

"Ok, Mom. I'm sorry you don't hear everything, but I would be glad to tell you what they say."

"When the new hearing aids come out, Dad wants to buy me one, and hopefully I'll be able to hear better then. Now, here we are at the church. The same gentleman is at the door, and he'll tell you where to go if you've forgotten. He seems very nice and he waves to me when you go into your class, and then he waves to me when you come out to meet me. I'll be right here outside this church by this tree. Now hurry up, or you'll be late."

"Ok, Mom. I'll hurry right up those steps, and I'll tell you the whole Bible story and the songs we sing when I come out. Take your walk around the block to keep warm. I love you, mom."

"I love you too, Joanie."

The man at the door in his blue suit, white shirt and red and blue tie told me where my class was meeting today, and I got in there and sat down just in time for the first song which was *I'll be a Sunbeam* (Nellie Talbot).

> Jesus wants me for a sunbeam to shine for Him each day.
> In every way try to please Him at home, at school, at play.
> A sunbeam, a sunbeam, Jesus wants me for a sunbeam;
> A sunbeam, a sunbeam, I'll be a sunbeam for Him.

"Hey, Mom. The teacher told us the story of how Jesus loves all the children in the world, and how He wants me and all the kids in my Sunday school class to be shiny sunbeams for Him. Let's hold hands and walk home slowly as it's not snowing anymore and the sun is shining. I was so happy to see you leaning against the tree waiting for me."

Mom in Detroit

A friend and Dad, WWI

CHAPTER 5

TIME FOR EVERYTHING

First Train Ride

I remember my first train ride very well. I'm not sure of my age, but it was before I started school. I always begged to go see my grandma.

Dad worked twelve hours a day, and did not have a vacation, leave time, sick leave, or unemployment benefits. If he worked, he received his pay at the end of the week in cash in a small brown envelope. If he did not work, he did not receive his pay in a small brown envelope. So my folks could not often drive me to Grandma's because she lived in another state.

After supper all of us on the fourteenth floor of our apartment building went out to play between the apartment buildings, but when it got dark, we had to go inside. We took our baths, cleaned up, and then were allowed to walk up to the roof of the building for an hour to play checkers, listen to the sounds of ships in the harbor and horns honking in the streets, gaze at the stars, and best of all, listen to the older kids tell stories. Some of the kids had taken a train to visit their relatives. It was fun to hear them tell stories about the conductor, the engineer, the businessmen, the moms with their children, the hoboes in the cattle cars, and the food they could buy through the windows when the train stopped at stations to let passengers come aboard.

Then the thought came to me. I could take the train by myself to visit my grandma. I kept telling my folks all about the train that went close to my grandma's house. They were not sure about it, but my dad went down to the train station to find out if it was safe for a child to go alone, and if the conductor would see that I got off at my grandma's place, which was next to the train track. It so happened the conductor knew the area, as bags of flour, sugar, and salt were dropped off there for the coal mining company store. Dad asked if they could send grocery boxes with me to take to my grandma. He told my dad that one box per window could be handed out to someone.

It was really exciting when my dad came home that evening. He had bought a ticket for me to visit my grandma! All my aunts and uncles brought food to pack in the boxes. I think there were twelve windows, so it was like Christmas packing the boxes with the many items you couldn't buy from the coal mining store.

The day finally arrived for me to board the train and go to my grandma's. My dad told the conductor the exact place where I was to be dropped off. He would see a clothesline just around the bend to the south, and a white sheet would be on it that he could not miss. The conductor reminded my dad that he knew the area of Clearfield County quite well. It was not an official stop, but the train would slow down, and he would see that I got off along with a box from every window. They shook hands, and my dad told him to come to the restaurant where he was chef for lunch when he returned to the city.

It was so much fun to ride on the train. I ran from car to car, but did not make it to the caboose, as the conductor said that it was not a nice place for little girls. I was on the train it seemed like forever, but finally the conductor said we were getting close and in another hour we should start looking for the white sheet on the clothesline. Everyone was so excited, and some of them even put their heads out the window to watch for the white sheet.

Finally the conductor hollered that this was the bend, and just as we chugged around the bend I looked out the window. More white sheets were hanging on the line than you could count! My grandmother had borrowed a sheet from every house in town to hang on the clothesline. The train came almost to a stop, and the neighbors reached for the boxes handed down to them from the windows. I stood behind the conductor in his black trousers, black tie, black spit-polished shoes, and white shirt. He reached down, picked me up gently, and set me down on the ground as my grandmother rushed toward me. Everyone on the train waved and shouted "Goodbye, Joanie! Have fun with your grandma!"

First Time Riding a Horse

My folks introduced me to horses before I was of school age. Every year we went to the Kentucky Derby in May and the Hialeah, Florida Flamingo Day in September. Both races were exciting because of all the people and the extra events leading up to the races.

The Kentucky Derby was a sight to behold, and it was exciting to watch the *Parade of Hats*. In my eyesight, the women were the most beautiful women in the world, but my dad used to say to my mother, "Does a fancy, expensive hat improve your luck in picking winners?" Everyone had roses, as the official flower of the Derby was a red rose. The winning jockey received a bouquet of sixty long-stemmed roses wrapped in ten yards of ribbon. I would think to myself, "Why do they give roses to a man?" My dad said it was tradition. One year my dad knew the jockey who won and received the roses. He gave me one of his roses when we walked back to his stable after the race. I was in heaven, as it was the most beautiful rose I had ever seen in my life because roses don't grow in Florida. And it was all mine!

The Hialeah Flamingo Day was spectacular. It was called *the world's most beautiful racecourse*. The Flamingo Fountain was behind the grandstand. Hundreds of pink birds with extremely long legs and necks were wading in the fountain. Their thick bills bent sharply down in front, and their long legs trailed behind. It looked like the flamingos could easily fly backward as well as forward. Even during the announcements they made gooselike calls, gabbling away and honking. It was exciting when the jockeys made a grand entrance, riding their horses around the track. All the jockeys were dressed in flamingo pink, and their horses' special attire was pink from their manes to their toes. Everyone cheered as they all lined up in front of the grandstand before the race. It was a sight to behold.

My favorite thing was not watching the races, but going to the horse stables, meeting the jockey, and watching him take care of his horse. The jockeys talked to us as we walked from stable to stable. The jockeys were my size, and some of them were not as tall as me, even when I was in fourth and fifth grade. My dad loved horse racing and studied the history of the horses' winning streaks. I read some of the statistics to him when we sat on one of the benches outside the stables. The jockeys gave my dad some so-called "tips" on the horse they thought would win the race. Their tips did not always turn out to be what they predicted.

The horses always appeared clean and in good health. Their gear was always in good condition. One time we arrived earlier than usual. The jockey walked me over to his saddle and named all the features on the saddle. I wrote down the eleven names. Starting at the very top and going clockwise: the *Pommel, Twist, Seat, Cantle, Panel, Stirrup Iron, Saddle Flap, Stirrup Leather,* and at the very bottom: *Knee Roll, Stirrup Bar,* and finally the *Skirt.* My dad held me up so I could rub their furry manes, as that is where the jockey told me that they loved to be rubbed. Some of the stables had what they called *Schooling Shows,* but I thought they were play days. It was fun to watch all the kids compete in games and walk or trot the horses. The kids all wore leather chaps that matched their vests. The chaps kept their legs from getting chaffed. The one lesson I learned was that you had to have a lot of patience and compassion not only for the horse, but for the rider of the horse as well.

I used to go to the movie theatre on Saturday afternoons and see serials of *The Lone Ranger* who rode his horse, Silver. It was white, part Morgan and Arabian. His friend Tonto rode a Pinto that was gray and white, named Scout. Then Roy Rogers had a horse named Trigger, a Golden Palomino. One Saturday in place of the serials, the film *Tumbleweeds* played with Gene Autry riding his Morgan horse that had three white socks and white hairs down the front of his face. His horse was called Champion. Several times I saw a wild Appaloosa herd in the hills of Kentucky near Olive Hill where my dad lived as a young boy. They have striped hooves and a blotchy pattern of pigmented and non-pigmented skin. As a child, I would fantasize that I was riding on Silver, Scout, Champion, Trigger or a wild Appaloosa that I named Pal, with my hair blowing in the wind, galloping into the wild blue yonder.

My first experience on a horse was in Cleveland, Ohio when the third Saturday of every month a cowboy came with his horse to the apartment buildings near Euclid Avenue. I lived on the fourteenth floor. I watched for this cowboy every month, but especially this time because it was my birthday month, and I was going to ride a horse for the first time. I was so excited. I was first in line to stand by the corner of the apartment building. He gave me the chaps, vest, and hat to put on. I felt so important. Then he helped me put my left foot in the left stirrup iron and swing my right leg over to the other side where I slid my right foot into the right stirrup iron. Then he tightened the stirrup leather, and I held on to the pommel. I waved to my mother and all my friends standing in line. He walked with me around the block and took my picture. The ride cost 25¢. It was a lot of fun, but I didn't want it to end.

I was in high school before I went horse back riding again. This time we lived in St. Petersburg, Florida. Every Saturday morning seven of us went to the Orange Blossom Stables to go horse back riding through the orange and grapefruit groves. We stopped, picked an orange or a grapefruit and ate them while we were on our horses. We didn't peel the fruit. We took our index fingers and punctured a deep hole where we pulled the stems out. Then we squeezed in a rhythm with both hands, squirting the juice into our mouths. It tasted so good. We returned with our horses to the stable with sticky hands, face, and clothes. Even the seat of the saddle and pommel were sticky! The owner was nice. He had us hose down the horse as he wiped off the saddle. We ended a perfect day of riding with a hose-water fight.

First Job

I was ten years old and didn't have any money to go to the county fair outside of town. I knew my folks would give me money if I asked them, but I wanted my own money. I wondered what I could do to make some money. I was not old enough to sign up at the Social Security office. When I went down there, they told me to come back when I was twelve. That meant waiting two more years! Two years was a long time!

All this was going through my head as I stood between the restaurant where my folks worked and the town grocery store run by the Baker Family. The owners of the grocery store gave me one quarter when I straightened the cans on their shelves. The delivery truck came twice a month. I unpacked all the boxes and helped put them all away. They gave me two quarters for this, as it took a long time. They never asked me to help; it was something I wanted to do. Otherwise, I had nothing to do. It was a hot summer day with flies buzzing around. I didn't know why my folks wanted to live in the center of Florida, instead of next to the water. The flies down by the water didn't seem to annoy me so much.

Out of the store walked my favorite couple. They were flushed and wiping perspiration off their foreheads. I always thought they were close to a hundred years old because they had so many wrinkles. The man was almost bald, and you could see her scalp where her hair was thin and white. It took them a long time to walk back and forth to the store to get their groceries. They stopped and sat down on the bench in the park to rest for a few minutes and then continued on. They used to drive their car to the grocery store, but now he can't see as well. He felt bad when they didn't renew his license.

I had nothing to do, so I offered to carry their two bags of groceries home for them. They hesitated and said the bags were too heavy. I carried the bags, one in each arm, while we walked to their house. They had a nice little house with two palm trees in the front yard. We walked around to the back and went in by way of their screened-in porch. They invited me to stay for a glass of lemonade; I enjoyed it and drank two more glasses. When I left, they gave me a quarter. I was so excited that I almost forgot to say, "Thank You." As hot as it was with the sun beating down on my head, I skipped all the way back to the restaurant to tell my folks. They smiled, and my dad said, "Joanie, you just found yourself a job. You are now self employed!"

I stood outside the grocery store every day from then on and carried groceries home for shoppers. Sometimes I made a quarter. Sometimes I made fifteen cents. Sometimes I made a dime. Sometimes I made a nickel. I always said, "Thank You." I love making money for doing something I like to do. Best of all, I was self employed and could work when I wanted to, which was all the time. I didn't have to worry about competition. None of my school friends wanted to carry groceries home for anyone, let alone in hot weather.

One evening we were sitting on our screened-in front porch. My folks asked me what I was going to buy with all the money I was making now. Dad teased me and asked if he could borrow some, and he'd pay it back at the end of the week. My mother told me not to loan him any money, even though he said he would pay it back. I told them that I didn't have any money here at the house. They wondered where I'd hid it. I told them that I didn't hide it. Then Mother asked, " Where is it?"

"I go to the bank down the block. The man behind the counter helped me fill out a card. Every day when I go in with some money, he marks the amount on the card." I ran to my room and got my bankcard to show them. My folks were shocked. My balance was twenty-seven dollars and fifteen cents. Dad whistled through his teeth and said, "You have done well, Joanie. It has been only seven weeks!"

I kept carrying groceries for shoppers until we moved to another town. I loved my job and knew I'd miss it when we moved. Dad assured me that I would think up another job so I could make money wherever we lived, and I did.

Am I a Gambler?

Am I a gambler? I don't think so.

My first exposure to gambling was in Las Vegas, Nevada. It was during WWII. My dad was a chef. He was asked and offered a job at a VA Hospital in California. We were living in Michigan. My dad was a veteran from WWI and very patriotic. He felt he should do what he could to help the men who were wounded in action and sent home to recuperate. He accepted the job at the VA Hospital in California.

I was ten years old and in the fifth grade. Our family car was a green Plymouth coupe. The three of us sat in the front seat. Within a week we sold all our furniture, except my roll down desk, trombone and bicycle. We gave my desk to my cousin and my trombone to another cousin. My desk is still at my cousin's house in another state, and the trombone was passed on to one cousin after another till we lost track of it. No one was interested in learning to play it. My bicycle was tied onto the roof of the car. Everything we owned was stuffed in our Plymouth coupe.

We were given gas ration coupons that would take us to California, and then we were told we would be eligible for more. My uncle gave us two of his shoe ration coupons. He said we would have to do a lot of walking to find a place to live once we got there. We were leaving many relatives from both sides of the family, so there was quite a tearful farewell.

It seemed like we did not get very far each day. My mother read to us on and off all day from our one-volume encyclopedia. It was the only book we had, except for Dad's Masonic Bible that was blue with gold-trim pages; it did not have any pictures. All the names of my parent's sisters and brothers were written in the beginning pages with their birthdays beside their names. Two of Dad's brothers and two of Mom's sisters had died, so those dates were written beside their birthdays with a dash between the dates. That was strange to me. I never asked why they did it, but I wondered to myself why they didn't just write their names. Who cares about the dates?

It took almost two weeks to reach California. When Dad got tired of driving, we drove up and down the streets of a town and looked for a "Rooms for Rent" sign in the front yard of a house. It was fun staying in a home; the family was always nice and friendly. We got up early the next morning and drove on.

The only place we stayed two days was in Las Vegas. This was sort of a mini-vacation. Dad said it would be a long time before he would ever have a day off from work once he started, as a war was going on.

One day after breakfast, I sat all day and watched an old man in jeans, t-shirt, and cowboy boots play the slot machine. He put nickels in the slot machine and pulled the handle down and back up. Different kinds of fruit came up. If there were three of one kind in a row, he won some nickels. They rattled down into a catcher on the bottom of the machine. My dad and mother played other machines. They were laughing and winning once in awhile, but not every time. My dad gave me some nickels and told me to get up and put them in the machine. I took the nickels, but did not want to lose them. I kept putting it off and watched the old man put one nickel in after another. He was not winning. He took a break to have some lunch. While he was at lunch, I went up and looked at his machine with its pretty lights, but I didn't put my nickel in the slot. I wasn't quite ready.

The man came back and smiled at me, thinking I had put my nickels in the machine while he was eating lunch. He bought several rolls of nickels and kept playing and losing. Finally, he gave up in the late afternoon and walked out. My folks came over and sat by me. My dad was encouraging me to play at least once, as we would not be coming back again. I walked up very slowly to the machine the man had played. I didn't take all my nickels out of my pocket, just one. I put my nickel into the machine very slowly, and I could hear it go down. I thought I was ready to pull down the handle. My dad almost pulled it down for me, but my mother told him not to be so anxious and to let me do it.

I pulled down the handle and, to my surprise, more nickels came out than you could count! They were all over the floor, more nickels than my mother and I could carry out to the car in our skirts! We made two trips, dumping them on the floor behind the front seat. We came back in, and my dad wanted me to put my other nickels in the machines. I wouldn't do it. He kept coaxing me, but my mother told him that I was doing the right thing. I won, and I had lots of nickels. I was going to keep them. "This is a good way to be, and more people should do the same thing," she said. They should not lose everything they had won. Dad told my mother in the car that I wasn't a gambler. He told me that I did the right thing by stopping after I had won.

My next gambling experience was in Hialeah, Florida. My folks loved horse racing. I really didn't like horse racing. I liked to walk around the stalls where the horses were kept. It was fun to talk to the men that took care of the horses and the jockeys who wore colorful jockey outfits. My mother's brother and wife came to visit us all the way from Michigan. They wanted to go to the races, so off we went to the races. They didn't want to walk around the stalls with me; they wanted to bet on a horse to show. I didn't know what that meant. My aunt said it was a sure thing. We would make money on this horse to show. It cost two dollars. She wanted me to go in with her. We would split the prize money when the horse came in to show. I very reluctantly gave her one dollar. To me, one dollar was a lot of money. She went up to the window and placed the two-dollar bet. She came back, and we walked to the fence to watch the horses take off when the gong blared out. The mud was flying. I couldn't even see our to-show horse. The race was over in a very short time. The horse we put our money on did not show. I was very upset. I jumped up and down. My face was red. I complained, cried, shouted, and could not get over losing my dollar. My folks, uncle and aunt could not comfort me. They even offered to give me back my dollar. I didn't want their dollar! I wanted my dollar back!

My dad decided then and there that I was not a gambler. I should never again put money on a horse or play the machines. He said that you had to be able to lose. He told me I had to take it like a good soldier when I lost or won. Whatever that meant, "to take it like a good soldier," I did not understand. And I knew that I would never play at anything again that would take money from me. My mother said I made a good decision.

Am I a gambler? I don't think so.

Green Stamps

Oh, how I loved green stamps when I was a kid! Mom and I always shopped at the stores that gave you green stamps when you bought something. You glued the stamps onto the Green Stamp Book pages. We had more fun going through the Green Stamp Catalog to see all the stuff you could buy.

It was my job to lick the stamps and put them in the book. You would choose what you got with the stamps from their catalog. Each book would be big enough to hold 1200 stamps. This experience taught me how to count up to 1200, and then when we accumulated 8 or 10 books I practiced my multiplication by 1200 times 8 or 10. My folks were so proud of me that I could not only add like I was taught at school, but I could also now multiply.

One time we had enough books that were filled with stamps with the help of our neighbors to get a big 2-slice toaster. Then we would help the neighbors out when they needed just one or two books to get what they wanted. Another time we went together with three neighbors, combining our stamp books so we could get a hand operated ice cream maker. That ice cream maker lasted for over 5 years, my grandma told me, and it was used every Friday night all summer long. The older boys and their dads took turns cranking the ice cream freezer.

The only time I was there in the summer, they went to the barn to get the block of ice that was stored there from the dead of winter under the straw. I thought it was a miracle that the ice didn't melt away. I went with the men when they went to the barn, and I just knew it would be a small melted block. To my surprise, it wasn't small at all!

Another fun time we saved our books of stamps for the mother of my favorite girlfriend in my Sunday school class. She was going to have a baby, and she wanted a cradle that was on rockers so she could rock her new baby to sleep with her foot as she was still nursing her little girl. We were all excited about this cradle, as we thought for sure it was going to be just right for her new baby, which we just knew was going to be a sister for her little blond curly-headed sweet big sister. It didn't quite work out the way all of us kids had planned. The baby turned out to be a curly redhead boy who had colic.

Oh, collecting, gluing the stamps in the book, looking through the catalog book, and dreaming what you would like to get with your green stamps was a lot of fun for the whole family.

Pickle Jar

As far back as I can remember the pickle jar sat on the floor beside the dresser in my parents' bedroom. When Dad got ready for bed, he emptied his pockets and tossed his coins into the pickle jar.

As a small girl, I was always fascinated at the sound the coins made as they were dropped into the jar. They landed with a merry tinkle when the jar was almost empty. When the sun poured through the bedroom window and the jar was filled, all three of us sat at the kitchen table and rolled the coins before taking them to the bank.

Taking the coins to the bank was always a big production. Each and every time, as we drove to the bank, Dad said, "Those coins are going to help you go to college so you won't have to do manual labor like me. You're going to do so good, going on to college." We always celebrated each deposit by stopping for an ice cream cone. I always got chocolate. Dad always got vanilla. When the clerk at the ice cream parlor handed Dad his change, he showed me the few coins in his hand. "When we get home, we'll start filling the jar again." I always dropped the first coins into the empty pickle jar.

The pickle jar taught me all these qualities far better than the most flowery of words could have done. The little ole pickle jar played a big part in my life as a girl. It showed me how much my dad loved me. Dad always dropped his coins into the jar. Not a single dime was ever taken out. Dad looked across the table at me, pouring catsup over my beans to make them tastier. "When you finish college, Joanie, you will have a good job and buy anything you want to eat."

Sometimes we forget to count our blessings. Dad always said, "God puts us all in each other's lives to influence one another in some way, so look for God in everyone." Happy moments, praise God. Difficult moments, seek God. Quiet moments, worship God. Painful moments, trust God. Every moment, thank God.

Saving Money

What makes us save our money? When do we start? Especially in elementary school, I felt that all my friends had a weekly allowance. What did they spend their money on? Did anyone ever think to save their money so they could buy something big like a bicycle or a pair of roller skates?

When I was young, it seemed like everyone got his or her allowance on a Saturday morning. Right away they went to the dime store or the neighborhood grocery store to spend it on candy or an ice cream cone. Some boys went all the way and got double dips. The dips were very big, and you had to hurry and lick fast, as it had chunks of ice cream hanging down the sides. The girls, for some reason, always had one dip. For a penny, you could have it dipped in the bowl of colored sprinkles. The popular candy then was small, different-colored, round drops half the size of a dime on a long narrow strip of paper. You peeled them off one by one. For a nickel, you walked away with a bag of candy that contained a strip of colored drops, a big sticky caramel sucker, a licorice pipe, a square walnetto wrapped in cellophane paper, a ribbon candy, and sometimes the grocery man would throw in a stick of Juicy Fruit Gum or Black Jack Gum. By this time everyone had no nickel to spare, as it was movie time at one o'clock in the afternoon. Movies cost a nickel on Saturday and a dime on Sunday, so everyone pooled his or her money. One of the boys drew two circles in the dirt. One was for the girls, and one was for the boys. We threw the penny we had left into the circle. It always seemed to work out that there were five pennies in each circle. The girls always went for Nesbit Orange or Coca Cola. I never bought any candy or soda pop of any kind. I did not have a sweet tooth. So I was able to save my money when we all tramped down to the dime store or grocery store. The boys all shared one bottle of Coca Cola, Pepsi, or an RC. It usually wound up to be Pepsi because it was twelve ounces and went farther. They chanted:

> Pepsi Cola hits the spot
> Twelve ounce bottle that's a lot
> All this for a nickel too
> Pepsi Cola is the drink for you.

Movie time on Saturday was a fun time to get together. We all met at the big park in our neighborhood and walked to town, twenty-two blocks. A few in our group got tired walking and caught the trolley that cost a nickel. The walkers met up with them at the benches in front of the movie theatre. Two of my classmates and I never took the trolley, as we did not want to spend our nickels. My mother always gave me two nickels for the trolley, a nickel for the movie, and a nickel to spend. Everyone went into the movie theatre, but me. I sat outside on the grass with my back to the theatre building and waited for my friends to come out. They coaxed me to go in by telling me about the *Porky Pig Cartoons* and *The Lone Ranger and Tonto* episodes. For some reason, whatever it was, I did not want to spend my nickels. When they all sauntered out, I quizzed them about what had happened to the Lone Ranger and about the cartoon that played this week. Most everyone walked home because they'd spent all their nickels at the candy counter in the theatre.

I hurried to get home, so I could tell my mother all about the movies. We sat in the front screened-in porch on the white, bamboo chairs and laughed and laughed, as I told all about the cartoon and what happened to the Lone Ranger and Tonto. Then I changed clothes and went for a swim in the Big Bayou, while my mother fixed dinner. But before I left to go swimming, I put my nickels in the first drawer of my five-drawer dresser in my bedroom.

This weekend routine went on until I was in junior high school. I went with my friends every Saturday, but never rode the trolley or went to the movies, and I kept putting my nickels in the top shelf of my dresser drawer. By the time I was in junior high, I had figured out a job for myself. This was my very first job. I went down to the local neighborhood grocery store and stood outside, asking the older folks if they would like me to carry their groceries home. It surprised them at first, but after awhile I had regular customers. They gave me a tip. Sometimes it was a nickel, sometimes it was a dime, and occasionally it was a quarter, but that was only around a holiday. It did not happen often. I enjoyed carrying bags of groceries for the folks, and they said they enjoyed having me help them.

One day my mother said she got the shock of her life. She was cleaning and polishing the little bit of furniture I had in my bedroom, and the top drawer of my dresser was slightly opened. As she went to close it, she had to use both hands, as it was heavy. She opened it and saw all the change! I never counted it, but it was a lot. I just saved it. So when I came home that day, she confronted me quite emotionally, as she thought I had stolen some money. I told her that I had saved it. Then I told her about the movies and other functions she'd given me money to go to with my friends. It was hard for her to believe I saved all that money. She questioned my friends the following week, and she even had my dad question the theatre manager. Of course, I had told the truth. My dad and mother asked me what made me save my money, and what I was saving it for. They were both in a state of shock. They told the story to all my aunts and uncles. I think it was one of their favorite stories about me.

I don't know what made me save the money at first; I just liked saving it. I didn't want a bicycle or a pair of roller skates; I had a bicycle and a pair of roller skates. I used to go by the RCA store and listen to Beethoven music on records. The stores then had an RCA dog sculpture standing outside. I also liked to visit the camera store. I decided that someday I wanted a Victrola phonograph you had to wind by hand and a camera. My dad and mother thought it would be good for me to start a savings account at the bank in town. So my mother walked me to the bank with my change in a couple of grocery bags we carried, and the teller at the bank had me sit at her office desk with her and count my money. She was quite taken aback with all the change and the story behind it that my mother told her.

I was most fortunate no one had to tell me how to save money, or when to start saving. I just did it. It began when I was in elementary school. Before I was out of junior high school, I had a 35-millimeter Agfa camera and a Victrola phonograph with Beethoven records I bought with the money I saved. I still had money in my bank account, and the same lady helped me count my change every time I went to deposit my money in the bank.

Drugstore

One afternoon I was walking home from elementary school on a hot, humid day. As I passed the front of the drugstore, I read a sign that said, "Soda Jerk Wanted". I had no idea what a soda jerk was, but I didn't care, as it was a good excuse to go into the store. It had ceiling fans and would be cooler than where I stood looking in the window.

I was fascinated with this drugstore. It had a jukebox with a couple dozen songs, a marble counter with a mirror on the wall behind it, and brightly colored stools that spun round and round. The drugstore soda fountain served ice cream cones dipped in sprinkled, colorful candy, sodas, milk and malted shakes, sundaes, banana splits with cherries on top, cherry coke, root beer, and all flavors of ice cream and syrups. All these choices cost only a nickel or a dime.

As I stood looking at everything, with no money to buy anything, the owner came up to me and asked me what I wanted. I told him I was hot and not only wanted to cool off, but also wanted to know if I could be a soda jerk. He smiled and asked me to sit down at the counter. His wife gave me a tall glass of root beer. She said it was "on the house." I didn't know what that meant, but I drank it. I was tall for my age, and I'm sure they didn't know how young I was. I didn't tell them either. The owner asked me lots of questions. Evidently I answered them correctly because then he said, "Would you like to be a soda jerk and work two hours right after school every day?" I was overcome with joy, but I had to ask him, "What is a soda jerk and what do they do?" He said that a soda jerk was a person like you and me. You work behind the counter and wait on the people who come in and sit down on the stools. You make ice cream sodas mostly, as that is our biggest seller. You put syrup flavoring in a tall glass and add carbonated water, plus two big scoops of ice cream. You serve the sodas with special long-handled spoons and straws. Special glasses are used for sundaes, shakes, and banana splits. When you finish your two-hour shift, you can have your choice of any ice cream selection.

I was really excited and he told me to ask my mom and dad. If they gave their permission, I was to come after school next Monday for my first day of work as a soda jerk in the best drugstore in town. I ran the rest of the way home, bolted in the back door, and told my mom everything. She said we must ask dad before she gave her approval. My dad was all for it, as long as the work was not too hard for me. I started work the following Monday, worked 5 days a week after school, and made an average of two dollars a week in tips, plus I was so glad to work in a cool place.

Do I like ice cream sodas, shakes, and sundaes? No, I don't. I enjoy an ice cream cone once in a while. I received a bonus at the end of the month for "not eating them out of house and home."

Early Working Girl

I really liked to work, and worked for whoever would hire me. Being tall for my age, no one asked me how old I was, which was a good thing, as I was underage. One summer I worked at the Traymore cafeteria in downtown St. Petersburg. They put me behind the counter serving food. For some reason they placed me in the spot of serving potatoes fried or mashed. I was told how many scoops to serve but I always gave a little extra, and that made old folks smile with a wink. It was long days with one hour break between breakfast and dinner and one half hour between lunch and dinner. I would always walk down to the beach, take my shoes and socks off and walk along the shoreline.

Between sixth and seventh grades I got a job as a carhop. I asked them which shift had more customers. The owner told me that customers always came in after a day's work and later on in the evening cars would swing in. So I took the shift from six in the evening till midnight. He was right. I was supposed to get a half hour break, but it never happened. I was told that I served an average of 40 to 50 cars a night. It was non-stop. The only relief I had was waiting for the trays to come through the window. Then I drank a glass of water without ice. I never took ice in my glass because then you had less water to drink. If you served over 30 cars you received an award of one dollar. I not only received a dollar every night but I made the most in tips. When I first started, the girls didn't want to share their tips so I said OK. It wasn't long before they changed their minds, but it was too late as I was making more in tips than all of them.

One winter the manager of the local movie theatre asked me if I would like to have a job on Friday and Saturday afternoons and evenings collecting movie tickets inside the theatre. The bonus was that I could come any other day I wanted and bring one friend to watch any movie. I had a good time collecting tickets and greeting all the families and friends. I enjoyed bringing some friends from large families in my neighborhood to go to the movie theatre. I really liked the job when it was bad weather, but in nice weather, which it was most of the time in the south, I could hardly wait to get outside. So after six months I decided that this was not the job for me.

One of my favorite jobs was the candy store at Webb's City. I wore my first uniform for work. It was a light gray, short sleeve dress trimmed in pink and a pink ruffled apron. I don't have a sweet tooth, so all the variety of candy was not tempting, but others who worked there really ate all the different selections of candy. It was a fun place to work! Many friends and neighbors walked around the candy counter many times deciding what they wanted to buy. During this time the samples on plates high atop the counter emptied fast!

Television and Air Conditioners

On my way to school one morning, I walked by a store with a sign in the window advertising a part time job for just the right person to sell televisions and air conditioners. This fascinated me. I didn't know anything about air conditioners and televisions. I had never seen an air conditioner and the only television I ever watched was a small screen set in a big piece of furniture at my aunt and uncle's home. After studying that sign, I had to rush to get to school on time, so I spent a nickel and caught the city trolley. But I thought about this job all day at school. The classrooms were so hot, and I thought maybe if I could get that job I could sell the school some air conditioners. My classmates told me to dream on, that they would only hire high school students. I made up my mind to try anyway on my way home from school!

On the way home from school I looked in the window of the store. They had two York air conditioners set up in the window for customers to look at and one above the door that was working. I walked into the small store. They had three small black and white RCA television sets on table stands with three chairs next to the opposite wall for customers to sit down and watch a program. The owner walked out from behind the back curtain and welcomed me into his new store.

We started talking and I told him that I knew about and had been to York, Pennsylvania and that it was a beautiful place, but I didn't know they made air conditioners, and I thought it would be wonderful to have an air conditioner in my classroom at school with one of his television sets, so all of the class could see the educational program that everyone on the news talked about every day. He poured a glass of Kool-Aid for each of us that he had mixed with powdered sugar, which was a real treat for me, as my mom didn't like what she called 'artificial drinks'. I slurped my glass of Kool-Aid down in seconds, as I was so thirsty and still warm. He took out a packet from his pocket and before he drank his Kool-Aid, he popped an orange-flavored chewable Aspirin into it, as he had a slight headache. He offered me one, but I told him I didn't remember ever having a headache. He told me that I was fortunate.

"You know where I would place that television set if this were my store?"

He smiled and said, "Where?"

"I would turn it on and put it in the window facing the people who walk by the store. I think you would really get folks to watch it, and you would sell more than you have in stock right now."

"Ok, and where would you place the air conditioners?"

"I would put one in the class at the high school that had the poorest attendance, and I bet the kids would seldom miss that class."

"You have good ideas." He walked over and took his sign out of the window and said, "Would you like this part-time job?"

"Yes!" I started work the next day after school.

Gadgets for Everyone

It was the 1940's when I first saw a picture on TV. Before that I had only listened to a radio with my folks. We loved sitting close to our radio and listening to the news for dad, baseball games for mother, and comedy for me. I sat on my dad's lap and the three of us laughed and talked as we listened to the radio.

Then my uncle bought a television. He was the first in the neighborhood to have one, and I was told not to touch it or put anything on it because it was very expensive. It had a really small screen, only 10 inches wide diagonally, and was in a big shiny, heavy, brown wood cabinet. I thought it was beautiful and that surely God made this gadget so people could learn more about the world. When the TV was first turned on, a test pattern broadcast before and after the station signed on. There was only one station. Sometimes it was fuzzy, but it was exciting to see a clear picture. I saw only a couple of programs in the evening. Other kids from the neighborhood came, and we all sat on the floor. We were well behaved and only watched the TV for an hour or so. Then we had to go home, as it was time for bed. We all wanted to stay longer, but only adults stayed late till the programs were over, which was about ten-thirty in the evening.

It was fun watching a game show. We pretended we were being asked the questions. One of us sometimes blurted out the answer before we heard it from someone in the audience on the TV. All of us checked our mailboxes right away when we got home from school, hoping we got a letter asking us to be on the TV game show. It never happened, but we still checked our mailboxes. We even asked our mailman if he'd bring it to our school during recess if we got a letter. He smiled and said he would bring it to us, and he'd come home early to watch us on TV too. Of course this never happened, but we never lost our hope and enthusiasm either.

Three years later one of the neighbors bought a 2-inch larger screen TV. Her husband made a shelf and placed the TV on it in his living room window. His yard was packed with kids sitting on the grass with their pillows and blankets watching TV! Outside we talked softly during the programs. We were careful not to be rowdy. The dad came outside on the porch once in a while to look around and check on us. No one was ever told to leave for bad behavior. We took turns weekly, writing a thank you note to him. Everyone signed it to thank the family for letting us watch programs on their television.

I was excited when my aunt was the first one in the family to have a telephone. She let us all use it once a day. It was a black telephone that sat on a corner table in the living room. We first dialed a word prefix and then four numbers. It was a party line, and my cousins and I listened in on other conversations till my aunt discovered what we were doing and took the black telephone. She put it back in its cradle.

My dad said, "What's going to be next? We have a radio. We have a television and a telephone. What else do we need? We don't have to invent anything else. We have it all!" Six weeks later out came the tape recorder! We were never the first family to get the latest gadget, but we were never left out. Everyone shared in those days.

Stingrays

My mother and I always looked forward to winter tourist season in Florida. Dad always seemed to get a job that was a seven-day week, with no time off and long days. So mom and I went to the beach often, enjoying the sunshine and watching fishing boats come in at dusk to sell their fish. I listened intently to many fish stories. One exciting tale was about catching stingrays. They were very common in those waters, and you could watch them from the shoreline, as they concealed themselves by hiding beneath the sand in the water. Most of the time they gave themselves away with their tail and eyes visible, while the rest of their flattened body took on the color of the sand.

One of the lifeguards approached my mother and I and pointed to where there were several stingrays. He told us to stomp and shuffle our feet while walking around in shallow water and they will go away, as they do not attack people. There were two incidents of stingrays using their tails to sting people. Their tails protect them, but it's very uncomfortable for the person they sting and sometimes leads to a trip to the hospital depending on the cut or wound. People really scream when the venom comes out of the grooves of the venom glands. I always thought the stingray was curious, as his eyes looked like they were cross-eyed or half asleep. Most of the time they moved slowly and looked very sleepy. But they really are alert and protective.

I went out one night with my friends whose dads were fishermen. It was a lovely full-moon night, and we saw the stingrays. The dads gave us long poles with sharp metal spears on the ends. It was supposed to be a game to see how many we could spear. It was easy to spear them, as they did not run away. We had to spear them and then hold them way up in the air and watch them wiggle. This was hard on me. They took our poles and shoved the stingrays off onto the supply boat that our boat was tied to. My friend's dad said he'd fix them for us for dinner the next day, which he did. He showed us how to cut them up. We could only eat the meat around the eyes and liver. The rest was too rubbery. It was a lovely dinner, and it tasted good, but I didn't take seconds when the platter came around the second time.

I decided this wasn't a fun sport for me. I didn't like spearing the stingrays.

I never went out again with my friends to spear stingrays. They teased and begged me to join them again and again, but it just wasn't the right activity for me. I think my folks were glad I made this decision on my own.

Jellyfish

"Watch out, Mom! Do you see all those sea jellies?"

"Yes, I see them, and I remembered to bring sunblock-jellyfish-sting-protective lotion. I hope we never have to use it! I was glad we had it last week when two children walked right into where the jellies were."

"Look over there! The warning sign tells us that there are a lot of sea jellies!" Jellyfish are shapeless blobs when you see them washed up on the shore, but they are dangerous when you see them afloat in the water. They say they have no brain, but I think they are smart the way they get around. Today there are a lot of them in all sizes. When their tentacles touch something, they let out their poisons right away. Their stings hurt a lot. Lifeguards have good lotions, but the sting causes pain on your skin that turns red and you get a bad rash.

Mom and I were very careful not to get too close, but we had fun watching them, as they looked like they were going sideways sometimes. We talked to one of the lifeguards, and he told us all about jellyfish. He said they were carnivores. I didn't know what he meant, so he explained that they eat small fish, dead or alive, and eggs. Their natural prey is the sea turtle. I was so interested in all he was telling us. Mom thanked him and we walked way down to the other side of the beach where it was safe to go in and jump the waves. We didn't want to worry about running into a school of sea jellies again.

The time always went fast when we were at the beach and before we knew it, we were packing up to catch the bus back home. All of a sudden we heard some shouting and saw the lifeguard running down to the shore where some people were gathered around two young boys who were crying and jumping up and down. They both had stings on their lower legs. One of the swimmers ran and got a bottle of salt water to rinse away the tentacles. The lifeguard had tweezers in his kit to peel off the tentacles. The boys finally calmed down and went up to the first aid house to shower using hot water. The lifeguard put vinegar on their legs.

In all the excitement, we missed the bus, so my mom and I sat comfortably on the green bench waiting for the next bus and talked about how thankful we were that we were able to avoid the jellyfish known to us as sea jellies. I fell asleep on the bus ride home. Once home, we showered, changed clothes, and I set the table for our evening meal, mom's always-supper-time-feast.

May I Have This Dance?

Our Toy Manchester Terrier could hear the motor of my dad's car when it was two blocks from the house. As soon as he started dancing around, my mother knew that Dad would walk through the side door of the garage to the living room within a couple of minutes. She rushed into their bedroom, changed her dress, took out her metal curlers, brushed her hair, and smeared a dab of lipstick on her lips.

Dad walked in the door, gave our dog, Toy, a bone from his jacket pocket, hugged Mom and me, took off his jacket, handed it to mom, leaned over close to her and said, "May I have this dance?" She smiled and took his hand, as I ran before them into the living room and turned the radio on to the same station every night, WSUN 620, located on the second floor of the Million Dollar Pier in St. Petersburg, Florida. It's the same radio station my mom and I listened to every day to hear the program *Don't Forget the Family Prayer- Jesus Wants To Meet You There*. That title was also a song sung by the trio Pearl, Audress, and Barbara Leaming. The trio's Dad, Charles M. Leaming, pastor of Faith Temple on 5th Avenue South, gave the daily devotional.

It wasn't a rule, but Mom and Dad always danced to three songs. After that, I tapped on one of their backs and said, "May I have this dance?" If I tapped on my dad's back, I danced with my mother. If I tapped on my mom's back, I danced with my father. Dancing didn't come natural to me, but they did their best to pretend I was dancing okay. I stepped on their toes all the time! After dancing a couple of times with my mom and my dad, I sat on the arm of the sofa and watched them. They laughed, talked low so I couldn't hear them, smiled, and winked at me.

Then Dad announced it would be the last dance. This was special because after a few seconds, they motioned for me to join them. I took off my shoes, stood on Dad's shoes, and held onto the belt loops of his trousers. Mom and Dad still hugged each other and said very loving things to each other and to me. When the music was over, we all hugged each other, said good night, and got ready for bed. Mother sat on the side of the bed and had me say a prayer. Dad walked by and both of them said together, "Good night, Joanie dear. I love you."

Aunt Catherine and Me
in Cleveland

Dad, Me and Mom in St.
Petersburg, Florida

CHAPTER 6

EVER CHALLENGED

Webb's City

Webb's City Drug Store, in St. Petersburg, Florida was between 7th Street and 10th Street. It covered seven blocks. It was more fun going there than to a carnival or a three ring circus. It was called The World's Most Unusual Drug Store, and the owner was James Earl "Doc" Webb, a patent medicine man. It had everything you could possibly want. To get there from our house, we jumped the trolley or bus for 5 cents or walked the 22 blocks. I usually walked because I would rather spend my 5 cents on a lot of other things. I joined many classmates from school every Saturday. We pooled our money and bought nickel cokes and 9-cent hot dogs. When one of us had a birthday, everyone chipped in and bought a giant soft ice cream cone for 10 cents for the birthday person who had to share by letting everyone get a small lick of the ice cream.

We could not take in everything in one day. We did as much as we possibly could do. I liked tossing money into the slots of the animal feeding machines. Sometimes a chicken would come out and dance, and then it would peck at a button and out would come food. When my mother went grocery shopping at Webb's City, Dad could choose the barber he liked best, as there were 26 barbers who would give him a haircut for 14 cents on a special day. The attendant saw me, and he gave me a free coupon for a double dip ice cream cone dipped in colorful sprinkles. I really liked the 14th floor of Webb's City, as it was a toy haven. Along with all the toys, a live mermaid danced and a bunny hopped in and out of the windows of a make-believe rabbit house. The bunny show had three acts. I went back two or three times a day to watch them perform. They served warm donuts that you bought 2 for 5 cents. If there were three of us, they usually gave us three for the price of two.

The floors were made of wood slats, and we used to see who could make the most noise, as they sounded creaky when you walked on them. The candy counter was on the first floor. They gave out many samples. Nutty fudge was to die for! Webb's City Drug Store had everything you could possibly want such as drugs, groceries, gas, hardware, furniture, haircuts, plants, clothing, dry cleaning, and an Arthur Murray studio that taught dancing on the roof. You name it, it had it.

The month of December we rode back and forth from Webb's City Drug Store to Doc Webb's house. His front yard was transformed into a *life size three ring circus* complete with life size elephants, zebras, clowns & high wire acts. It was amazing. Everyone loved Webb's City Drug Store.

Let's Go to the Movies

It was finally Saturday morning. I never thought it would arrive! Five days of school sometimes felt like a month. I always looked forward to weekends to get together with all my friends in the neighborhood and go to movies. Movies were 5¢ on Saturday and 10¢ on Sunday. Even though I loved to save my nickels and dimes, I occasionally went into the theatre with all my friends and watched whatever was on that day.

Saturdays we saw two movies, one right after another, and a cartoon. My favorite serial star was Tonto, the Lone Ranger's friend. Tonto called the Lone Ranger *Kemo Sabe*, which means faithful scout. My favorite cartoon was Donald Duck. I thought he was cute because he was a white duck with a yellow-orange bill, legs, and feet. He wore a sailor shirt with a red bow tie. His explosive temper was very funny.

Everyone in our neighborhood met where the alley meets the street, and each one kept just enough money to get into the movie theatre. We all pooled our resources for the kids that didn't have enough money. If we didn't have enough for them, we all went down to the ice cream shop and went from table to table asking for pennies till we had enough for everyone to go to the movies. Customers in the ice cream shop were most kind and laughed and teased us. We were well liked and our "gang" always helped each other.

We all walked to the movie theatre even though we could take the bus for 5¢. Just a few kids rode the bus. They waved and hollered at us walkers as they hung out the windows of the hot and stuffy bus. It was a long hot walk, but everyone was happy to be going to the movies. We took turns walking arm in arm with each other. Rosie was the first to have a boyfriend. She wore a big red bow in her curly, pitch-black hair, and her boyfriend Mike slicked back his straight, black hair till it made him look like one of the bad guys in the movies. They held hands and got teased a lot.

When we walked up to the theatre window, it took the cashier about 30 minutes to count all our change, give us tickets, and let us through the door. The first ones in saved the seats so we could all sit together. We were a fun group. We laughed and talked when we should have been quiet. We were never reprimanded, but the usher had a flashlight that he shined on us sometimes.

When the movies were over, we jumped, skipped, and ran home, as by this time we were all hungry. No one was left behind, as the older ones looked after the younger ones. We all arrived home at the same time. It was a good day, and tomorrow most of us would go the movies again, if we wanted to spend our 10¢, or we'd save it till the next weekend.

First Kiss

"Hey, Morrisey! Where are you going today? Who is going with you?"

"I'm not sure," said Morrisey.

"Where should we all go today? I usually like to go to the Henry Ford Plant and sit on the fence. Then you can see the model cars being painted."

The neighbor next door to my aunt's house was the boss of the River Rouge Ford Plant. He didn't mind all the neighborhood kids sitting on the fence. I was fascinated with the jabbering, paint spraying, and cars rolling out and being parked according to their color.

Morrisey said, "OK, let's go to the plant. I'll round up the fellas, and you get your girlfriends to come. We'll have a good time. Be sure and tell your mom where we're going. Our moms get upset when they don't know what's going on. Meet you in twenty minutes by O'Reilly's garage!"

This was going to be fun. It took about an hour to walk to the plant, sometimes longer. It all depended on how much horsing around went on between fellas teasing girls who fancied them.

I secretly dreamed about Morrisey holding my hand or even someday kissing me. Sometimes I felt ugly because I had freckles and a birthmark on my leg. My parents and all my aunts and uncles told me that I was pretty. But it wasn't my parents, aunts and uncles that I wanted to hear say that I was pretty. I wanted Morrisey to say it. But no such luck. It seemed like forever since I knew him, and he'd never said it.

Four of our mothers were in the house canning cherries. I hated canning anything! Canning meant swatting gnats that came out of nowhere to annoy you. If you didn't can, you wouldn't see and be bothered with those pesky creatures. I didn't know why they didn't figure that out! I caught on right away! No canning, no gnats. What is so hard about that? Why couldn't our mothers just buy the fruit they wanted in cans at Mr. Pagone's grocery store? No, they had to use the fruit God allowed to grow. You just couldn't convince them how nice it would be without those gnats. Cherries weren't that great anyway. When our mothers waved "good-bye," they always told us to be home in time to clean up for dinner before our dads came home from work, because when they came home, they had the rights to the bathroom. They took showers, had a cup of coffee and sat down to read the newspaper until they were asked to come to the table.

Finally, we all met by O'Reilly's garage and were on our way. We hooped, hollered, laughed, and shoved each other. We had many shortcuts to get to the plant. We crossed over the railroad tracks, took our shoes off, and waded through the stream. We climbed over neighborhood fences; sometimes the people hollered at us, but we just kept running and laughing. The most difficult and last shortcut was the entrance to the plant. We didn't want the guards to notice us, so we stood behind and beside big trees, and one by one we sneaked past the guards. Then we hoisted each other up to the top of the fence. We each sat in our favorite spot. I sat by Morrisey. I was always excited when he sat next to me. He was the leader of the group. I thought he was cool.

We were always late getting out of the plant area and had to run most of the way home. No one had a watch, which was always our excuse. When we stopped to get our breath, Morrisey's feet had blisters from his new shoes. Buddy carried him on his back, and that was the end of running for the three of us. The rest went on, but I stayed behind to walk with Morrisey and Buddy.

Just before we rounded the corner to our street, Morrisey said, "Hey, Joanie, lean over here." He kissed me. It didn't last very long, but I was in heaven.

"O Morrisey, I liked your kiss. Let's do it again sometime."

"Ok," he said. " I liked it too. It took me a long time to get up the courage. I knew you wouldn't hit me for kissing you when I was being carried on Buddy's back!" This was the best day of my life.

Twenty years later I met up with Morrisey at Buddy's birthday party. I walked in with my girlfriend, and he came over right away. He said, "Don't you owe me a kiss?"

I said, "I think so," and he kissed me again. This one lasted a little longer.

Southern Mrs. Bailey

Mrs. Bailey was the epitome of a very lovely southern lady. She was the teacher in the school down by the Big Bayou. Sometimes it was easy to get sloppy in the South, as it was always hot. Yet Mrs. Bailey always wore proper shoes, bracelets, and pearl necklaces. Girls wore dresses then, but the boys who were children of tourists or farmers, faces burnt by the sun and red necks, sometimes wore pajamas underneath their overalls, as it was often cold in the mornings. When the boys got out of hand, she walked over to them and treated them like gentlemen. She never shouted. Every morning she led us in the *Pledge of Allegiance to the Flag*, and we sang *God Bless America*. A different student read from the Bible, and she said a prayer. Her mannerisms, her lovely speech, the way she handled misbehavior, and her encouragement of the students led us all to respect her. If we all had our daily work done, we had the choice of whether we wanted to go out to play at recess or listen to her read from the classics. I never remember a classmate going out to play. Everyone liked to hear her read. You could hear a pin drop.

One day she explained that we were going into another building, a larger school, with many classrooms where every subject was taught in a different classroom. She gave us advice that we'd meet other students who didn't have as nice manners as we had, but she expected us to be a shining example of the True South. She had taught us how to behave in the best way, as ladies and gentlemen. The last week of 6th grade at Lakewood Elementary School, Mrs. Bailey passed out a reading list that would equip us for 7th grade. We were to put a check mark in front of every book that we had read. Students who had every book checked went to the front of the class and each was given a certificate. There were quite a few. Then those who had read half the list stood, and they were given smaller certificates. There was not one student who was not given a certificate, except me. I had been a 6th grader in four schools before I went to Lakewood Elementary. I had never seen a reading list before. I didn't recognize the name of any of the books. Mrs. Bailey had me stay after class. She said that if my folks gave her permission, she would take me to the St. Petersburg Public Library in downtown St. Petersburg. She drove me home, and my mother was very happy that my teacher would take the time to take me to the library and introduce me to the librarian there.

It was fun going to the library with Mrs. Bailey. She showed me where the books were on the shelves. By the fifth or sixth book, I caught on to the letters and numbers on the spine and could then find them all, except one book that was on reserve. I had my list, and I read every day of summer vacation. If they'd offered 7th grade in the school with Mrs. Bailey, I would have stayed.

When I enrolled in 7th grade at Southside Junior High School, I had read every book on the list and three or four that weren't on the list. The librarian at the library called my 6th grade teacher. Mrs. Bailey sent me a congratulations card that said, "I knew you could do it, Joan!"

The 7th grade went well. Every subject was taught in a different classroom. That gave me a chance to get some fresh air when I moved from class to class.

I had high grades although we moved a couple of times. My dad was offered a job at one of the hotels in St. Petersburg for the winter, so I was late enrolling in 8th grade at Southside. But I was active in the band, orchestra, and Cube Hot Shots. I went to Friday night dances with one of my classmates. He came by my house, and we walked back and forth to the school. It was a good, fun year. Junior high school was a big deal for me, and I learned to love it, but I longed to be back in Mrs. Bailey's classroom.

When I Was 12 Years Old

What a fun, enthusiastic, exciting, energetic, comfortable, not-a-care-in-the-world, friendly, the-world-at-your-fingertips age to be, and it lasted for 365 days that year! My folks decided to live in St. Petersburg, Florida, called the "Sunshine City" because the sun shone every day. If the sun didn't shine, the local newspaper, *St. Petersburg Times*, gave you a free newspaper. I only remember getting a free newspaper once the entire time I lived there with my folks. I was so excited when the newspaper boy gave me my free newspaper! I safely tucked it away in my special box of cherished heirlooms on the top shelf of my tiny closet. The thought didn't cross my mind that newspapers deteriorate, turn yellow and brown, if not preserved well. In our non-air conditioned house, the average temperature was eighty degrees and above, on the coast of the Gulf of Mexico in the "sunshine city". I was so disappointed when I opened my special box of cherished heirlooms twenty years later!

St. Petersburg was also called the city of newlyweds and nearly deads. Later in my life, I thought that was funny because when I was in Bible college our classrooms were in the back of an evangelistic center near the famous Webb City Drug Store. When the older folks got married, they asked the president of the college to marry them, since there was no fee. As part of our class requirements, we observed the weddings to learn how to officiate. With the whole school in attendance, each wedding was a huge celebration! More marriages after the age of 60 than before the age of 60 were performed, and each one was a huge party. It was a blessing to the older people to have all us young people celebrate with them.

Our junior high school had Friday night dances. I had never gone to a dance before, and now I looked forward to them every Friday night. Several of my friends and I walked to the dance together. All the girls sat or stood on one side of the gym, and the boys usually just stood on the other side of the gym. PTA mothers made pink punch and cookies for refreshments. No cookies were left by the end of the third dance! The boys woofed down two or three at a time. I didn't care because I only liked cookies my mother made early every Monday morning. The third month of the Friday night dances, a brown-haired brown-eyed tall, skinny fellow named Roger asked me to dance. I was so nervous I could not answer him, but just walked with him to the dance floor. I forgot I didn't know how to dance! He caught on quickly and told me when to step forward, backwards, and sometimes he held his arm up, and I went under it. I had a lot of fun. We danced every dance. The last dance they turned the lights down, and he told me we could stand closer together for the last dance. We did, but it made me nervous. I'd never stood that close to a boy before, but I liked it when I got used to it. He even walked me home right to the front door of our screened porch. From that Friday night on, he came to my house, and we walked back and forth to the dances. He missed the trolley to his house by walking me home, but he said he didn't care. Friday night dances lasted through the three years of junior high school, and we never missed a one.

Classes at school became more interesting when I was twelve. Latin was a requirement and quite a challenge for me as I always messed up verb tenses. I was popular in English class, as the teacher would have me read my stories I wrote of all the places where I'd lived with my folks. My parents and I traveled from state to state and city to city for my dad to find work. I loved it. We were in the South somewhere in the winter and up north in the Midwest or the East Coast in the summer. During World War II we were on the West Coast as my dad worked as a chef in a VA Hospital. I seemed to do well in Math and Social Studies. Math didn't give me a thrill, but Social Studies got my attention, again because of all the places we'd lived. I joined the band, and they welcomed another saxophone player. All the rehearsals, marching practices, parades, and concerts kept my life full and exciting.

My favorite time of day was when school let out in the early afternoons due to the heat. I took the school bus home, as it was faster than walking. It left me off right at the alley by where we lived and within seconds I was home. I greeted my mother with a kiss on the cheek, changed into my purple and white two-piece swimsuit, jumped on my bicycle, and cycled down to the Big Bayou to swim. I was never the first one there as hard as I tried to be. We jumped off a long, rickety wooden dock, but we had to be careful as sharp-cutting mean barnacles grew on the sides of it. They could tear your flesh. Many showoffs have scars to this day that prove what barnacles can do! The refreshing, hilarious swim time lasted about two hours before we all found our way back home again, thoroughly exhausted.

Mother always had dinner ready and the table set in the kitchen corner by the screened-in window where a lovely yellow guava tree grew. She made many a jar of guava jelly. When you held up the jar in the sunlight, you could see right through it. Mother and I listened to the radio. I did my homework and by the time I finished, my dad had come home from work. Sometimes the three of us took a walk or we sat on our front screened-in porch and told each other about our day. Much exciting, enthusiastic, energetic, comfortable, not-a-care-in-the-world, friendly and the-world-at-your-fingertips wonderful fun lasted 365 days when I was 12 years old living in the "sunshine city".

V-J Day – The Biggest Party of All

We were living in Winter Haven, Florida when President Harry S. Truman declared September 2nd, 1945 the official V-J Day on board the battleship USS Missouri in Tokyo Bay. Three months earlier was V-E Day, but V-J Day was the official end of WWII.

I loved living in Winter Haven, called the "Chain of Lakes". It was the home of Cypress Gardens, and it had a fun theme park called Legoland Park, one of the largest Lego-themed parks in the world. Winter Haven's many freshwater lakes were a delight to me. I liked freshwater lake swimming much better than the salt water at beaches even though the beaches were within an hour from home.

It was exciting living in Winter Haven because we lived in renovated servants' quarters in the middle of an orange grove owned by Mr. and Mrs. Westfall. They were kind to us. Mrs. Westfall had a beautiful orchid dress made for me to wear on my birthday with silver bells on it, and she had a birthday party I will never forget. She invited all the children of the business owners and the children who worked in their orange groves. The long table was decorated in red, white, and blue. A huge cake with candles I was to blow out and a big tub of chocolate and vanilla ice cream sat on the table. Her kitchen maids wore starched, white dresses with full aprons and served us.

However, I remember the biggest party of my life as the day that was the official end of WWII, V-J Day. Everyone in town was on the main streets walking, shouting, singing, shaking hands, hugging, and patting each other on the shoulders. My dad had a small restaurant in town next to Baker's Grocery Store. It was packed until late at night. When no tables were available, folks took their plates outside and sat on the curb. Baker's Grocery Store had to finally close, as it ran out of all fresh food. We eventually closed, as we ran out of everything. Everyone shared what food they had from home. It was like an all-day picnic that did not end. The one and only theatre had a Charlie Chaplain film that they kept running over and over until the wee hours of the morning. It's the only time my parents and I saw a film together, as my dad always worked seven days a week.

The eight or nine songs I remember everyone singing were: *Bye Bye Blackbird, Kiss me Goodnight Sergeant Major, Lili Marlene, Shine on Harvest Moon, Slow Boat to China, This is the Army Mr. Jones, White Cliffs of Dover, Won't You Come Home Bill Bailey* and *We'll Meet Again.* The high school band performed for everyone when the sun went down. They jazzed some of those marches up to speed with everyone clapping and pounding their feet to the music.

It was a sweet experience to welcome the men home from the war. The whole town showed up at the train station. I don't think there was ever a dry eye at the station. Most of the soldiers walked out, but many were on crutches, canes, and gurneys. Last came the caskets carried by soldiers.

It was a precious experience living in a small town where everyone looked out and cared for each other. My dad and mother talked for years about how living in Winter Haven would always be close to their hearts because the people were so kind, loving, and thoughtful. I had been to many elementary schools before moving to Winter Haven, yet I was accepted as one of them right away and felt loved like I was family.

Within a few months of when WWII was over, I was able to buy one bottle of catsup for the first time in two years for my mom's birthday. To celebrate her birthday we walked to the local drugstore and put our nickels in the jukeboxes to play music. Even though it was a hot summer day, we both wore nylons, as it was a special occasion. Then we walked home. Mom had prepared potato salad, green string beans with potato and bacon. We never served ourselves from the stove. All food was placed in bowls or on platters and put on the table. I wrapped my 25 cents allowance for that week in newspaper that I had colored and gave it to my mom as a present. We said to each other, "Eeny. Meeny. Miney. Moe. Catch a Monkey by the Toe. If he hollers let him go. One, two, three and you pray for our meal." Mom was number three, and she prayed for our meal. A theatre was in town that showed only newsreels continuously. We were going to go for five cents each, but we were too tired after dinner. My dad came home, and he brought a small fresh coconut cake with candles on it. What a treat, as coconut was scarce in the stores! Dad had some left over at work, and he brought it home for us to enjoy.

The war was over. At first everybody partied and celebrated. Then big adjustments had to be made. When the soldiers left, they were boys. When they came back, they were men. They had to find work, and family relationships had to be renewed. People often found out they had to move to put their lives back together as reality set in. I saw all this happiness and sharing, and I felt secure. This was because Dad was now the chef at the Pass-a-Grill Beach VA hospital in St. Petersburg Beach, Florida. That is where Joe DiMaggio signed my autograph book when he thanked Dad for all the good meals he had while he was at the hospital recovering from the war. The biggest party of all was remembered for years to come.

Love Is Such a Funny Thing

Love is such a funny thing. It's something like a lizard.
It wraps itself around your heart and nibbles at your gizzard.

I learned this little saying when I was a teenager. It thrilled me so much to read it because a classmate in 7th grade wrote it in my autograph book that I still have today. I wondered why he wrote it to me. He never talked to me very much, but whenever I turned around at my desk, he looked up and smiled. I think his smile stuck with me all these years. The other day at the grocery store I turned around to read and compare the price of an item, and I saw this young fellow who looked just like my long-ago friend. He was with his mother, and he was smiling at me. He said, "Everyone tells me that I look like my Dad."

"Well, your dad must be good looking."

Out of the blue his dad turned around and said, "That is great to hear. I always wanted to be good looking."

For reasons unknown to me, I seem to notice his smile at many functions, such as in the work place, at family reunions, church, civic meetings, wherever I go. When people take your picture they always say "cheese" which means to smile at the camera. Today you can see the picture right away, and if someone is not smiling, they take the picture again. A smile is contagious. When someone smiles at you, you smile back. A friendly smile can change the attitude of a person in an instant.

My folks were arguing when I stormed in one day with my report card, and I exclaimed with great enthusiasm, "I have an A in every subject including my science class!" They changed their expression to wide-brimmed smiles. They shared my enthusiasm with wonderful smiles and hugs, and then they hugged each other. This was a turning point in my life, as I had just completed several surgeries and missed three months of school. It was a celebration time!

One day on the radio my mother heard a preacher say:

> You can smile when you can't say a word.
> You can smile when you cannot be heard.
> You can smile when it's cloudy or fair.
> You can smile anytime, anywhere.

Of course we all knew this saying of Mother's, so we all repeated it together several times which was customary, and we laughed until Dad said it was his turn now. He always said the following verse he'd learned from his sister:

> Let me give some comfort to someone in need.
> It can be a smile, nod, kind word or deed.
> If I can change a frown to a smile again,
> Then I will not have lived in vain.

So we all repeated his saying over and over again, because he always said his took longer to sink in. Mother always said that he left some of the words out, but he would deny it. By the time we repeated the two sayings over and over again with many laughs, holding each other's hands, forming a circle and dancing, we were ready to go on to other things before it was suppertime.

Every Friday night the school had a dance. I was not planning on going, as I went once with several girlfriends, and all we did was stand or sit next to the wall of the gym. The girls who had boyfriends danced together all evening. So I decided not to go again. I felt left out for some reason. Then it happened one day after band rehearsal. The tuba player with a big smile came up to me and asked me to the dance. I could hardly talk, I was so excited. He said he wanted to go to the dance, and he'd pick me up because he knew where I lived, and he'd take me home. I thought I was in heaven. My heart really pounded. Am I in love or what? What is love? His smile was contagious. A contagious smile must be the forerunner of love. That is what starts the "nibbling at your gizzard".

Let's Go Crabbing

Crabbing was one of the most fun things to do with my girlfriend. A Norwegian family lived next door to my friend's house. The man had a collapsible box crab trap made from steel wire and fully strung. All four sides went down to collapse flat in the water. He loaned us his trap and showed us how it worked. To manipulate it, we were to hold the tough string that was connected to the bottom and all four sides. He also loaned us his small propane stove. We were to put a narrow pot on top of it to boil the crab right after we caught them. We were excited to take turns catching them and eating them!

I had a friend whose grandpa, Mr. Henry W. Hibbs, had a wholesale fish business near the railroad pier. He shipped a thousand pounds a day, my dad told me. It was the oldest fish store in the city of St. Petersburg. So my friend and I took our crab trap and asked Mr. Hibbs if we could have a fish head for bait to catch crabs for our lunch. He was most kind and fun to talk with. He not only gave us a fish head, but he also wired it onto the bottom of the trap. Off we went, walking and skipping to the beach by the pier in town on our new adventure. We were so excited!

We took turns. One sat up on the wall, let the crab net down flat in the water, and pointed to where the crab was, and the other stood in the water to make sure the crab box was just right. The crabs came one by one and walked into the crab net. The one on the wall pulled it up and put it on the sidewalk. We turned on our stove and carefully picked up the crab, making sure his pincers wouldn't touch us. They were mean-looking and tried their best to latch on to us. We boiled one leg at a time. Then we put the rest in the pot to cook. It didn't take long. Folks dropped by and gave us good advice.

My friend and I caught several crabs that day with the fish-head bait, and we ate them all. We were told what to scrape out that was not good, but the white meat in the body was delicious. We kept some of the pincers to show our folks and friends, but we didn't keep them long, as they smelled bad. After this first experience, we went several times and always came home with delicious crabmeat, fun and exciting.

Wrong House

Hey… Hey… Hey… Hey… over there! What's the matter with that well dressed guy in the blue-flannel suit standing in the shade of the patio next to the garage? He's there so he can't be seen from the street. He's throwing rocks at the window on the second story of that brick house next to mine! Do you think he's on drugs or something?

"Hey… Hey… Hey, fella! What are you trying to do? Do you want to break a window or something? There's a big lake two blocks down the road, or a stream that runs beside the railroad tracks just about six blocks from here. Glass breaks, you know! You could have much more fun skimming water with the rocks, and you wouldn't break anything, or hurt anyone. Just what are you doing? Is it fun for you to throw rocks at the window upstairs in the next house to mine? How come you are not talking? All you do is glance at me, and keep throwing rocks. You missed the window many times which is good, but now the dogs are beginning to bark, and you are going to wake people up in this block!"

"Hey! Come on! Stop it! Tell me what you are up to, and I'll see if I can help you."

"Ok. I'll tell you why I'm throwing rocks at that window. My girlfriend lives in this house, and I want her to come down and talk to me. We had an argument today at work during break time, and she got mad and left me standing alone in the employee lounge. I might have raised my voice a little more than usual, but I was determined to make things right between us. After she stormed out, no one spoke to me, and they left the lounge without saying a word."

"Who is your girlfriend? Maybe I can talk to her, and help you out."

"Her name is Susie."

"Susie who?"

"Susie Calamari."

"Why, I know Susie Calamari, and her family. This isn't her house. She lives two streets over, and two blocks to the right."

"Oh!"

Saxophone and Trombone Lessons

I used to love to listen to Jim and Tommy, the Dorsey brothers, on the radio. My folks listened with me, and we sometimes sang along or danced to the music in the living room. I always said that I was going to learn to play the saxophone first because it was easier to carry. Then when I got older, I would take lessons on the trombone, so I could play both instruments in the school band. Three of the schools I attended gave free lessons if you owned the instrument, starting in the third grade. I really enjoyed getting out of class and walking down the hall to the music room. I took my time and stood outside the door before I knocked to be let in. The teacher knew it was my time when I knocked, and he ran his fingers up and down the piano keyboard, and called me in.

Lessons were fun, as the teacher played along with me. I practiced a little bit at home, but I went to the music store in town with my mom, and she bought me piano music of popular songs. The owner of the store showed me how to transpose it for the saxophone. It was easy for me because basically it was one space down or one line up. My teacher caught on to what I was doing, and he had me bring the sheet music in, and we played the tunes together.

Every three months there was a recital. I dreaded it. It was always in the evening, so my mom and I caught the bus to get to the studio. My dad came later in the car when he got off work. The studio was altogether different-looking when there was a recital. The music teacher and his wife greeted us at the door, and he escorted parents to their seats. The performers sat in chairs in a half circle on the stage. A vase of beautiful flowers sat on the piano. All of us were dressed in our very best clothes. Our teacher wore a suit. We walked up to a stand to announce the next person's selection, and the person before us announced what we were going to play. Before we played our piece, we had to tell the story of the composer who wrote the music. I received my first small Mozart trophy. I really felt important. My folks said I blushed when I was announced the winner of the trophy. They served cookies and punch at the end of the recital. Adults were served first, then the rest of us woofed down far more than one cookie. All went well, but I was relieved when it was over.

The three of us drove home, happy and chatting away about the recital. When I was ready for bed, my dad and mother hugged me and told me how proud they were of me for playing in the recital and that they looked forward to the next time. Next time I was in the beginning class for the trombone, so I got to play both saxophone and trombone. I worked my way up to first chair with my saxophone, but I never got higher than second chair with my trombone. I played in the marching band, orchestra, and Cube Hot Shots all through my public school years.

Baseball on the Forehead

I was in 7th grade when the P.E. teacher asked me if I wanted to play baseball with a mixed team. Because of moving so often, I'd never played sports of any kind, nor was I really interested in playing baseball. I enjoyed watching others play, but I still liked to ride my bicycle to the beach or to the local fresh water lake close to where we lived to jump the waves in the ocean or dog paddle and jump off the dock in the lake near my house. I always said I was not an athlete, but I was a good sport. I don't mind losing in any game, but when I won, sometimes it was a nice feeling.

I told the P.E. teacher that I was not a sports person, but she said she would like me to come out for the practice times and see if I might want to play. I went out and watched and before I decided even to consider playing baseball, she signaled me to come up to the bat and give it a try, so I did several times. Soon I caught on and hit the ball out to the left field, and sometimes I hit it so high that no one caught it. I did not like to play first, second or third baseman positions. The balls were thrown to the basemen too fast. I was placed at the shortstop a few times and began to feel comfortable.

Several times I caught the ball when the batter hit it hard, and the P.E. teacher always complimented me. That felt good, so I thought that maybe someday I'd be a good player for the team. So I joined the team and many afternoons after school I went to practice. Many times we watched movies of baseball games and discussed them. I didn't join the discussions, as I wanted to just get out there and play and do my very best. I always wanted my team to hurry up and win the game. Then we could go home and go swimming before it got dark. It didn't always work that way.

We played ten or twelve games during baseball season with other school teams in our area. My school was small, and we had a small band that played, as well as six or seven cheerleaders who did stunts. They cheered the baseball team, especially after a homerun. They whooped and hollered along with the drummers in the band.

At our next to the last game when we were ahead, one of the best batters was up. He hit that baseball, and the next thing I knew, I was knocked out and lying on the ground. When I opened my eyes, I didn't feel too bad, but I was carried off the field and had a splitting headache. The ball had hit me on the forehead. I recovered quite quickly, but never played baseball again. I told my mother I was sorry that I got hit, as I knew baseball was her favorite game. She said she'd go with me to watch school games, but she didn't want me to play baseball anymore. That was the end of my baseball career. It was a good and fun time, although relatively short.

A second time I was hit on the side of my head by an oar of a rowboat after an adventurous night of stabbing stingrays, holding them high up in the air and watching them wiggle. Another time I was shoved into the wall of the municipal swimming pool while floating on my back. My head hit the cement wall of the pool. In winter, we flooded the yards to make ice for skating, and I was on the tail end of the whipping rope and hit the tree full force. That knocked me out. Sports were never the safest place in the world for me.

Toward the end of 8th grade, the top of my head was turning purple and blue on some days. My doctor referred me to friend of his, a specialist at the University of Michigan in Ann Arbor. My aunt and uncle from Michigan drove down, and I went to Michigan to live with them in the summer and fall. It started with three or four operations in the summer. Then I had two or three in the fall and one in the winter sometimes. I flew by myself on Eastern Airlines between St. Petersburg and Detroit back and forth many times. I was the first one to fly in the family. During one of the flights I was on between Detroit and St. Petersburg, a blade came off the propeller of the airplane. I heard a horrific, loud sound, and thought I saw it go by. People were screaming and getting up from their seats. The stewardess had a difficult time getting them to sit down. We were in the air and you couldn't walk off the plane! The pilot's quiet calm voice assured everyone that we were safe and would be able to land with only one propeller. We did.

I attended Fordson High School in Michigan and St. Petersburg High School in Florida. One time when I was home in St. Petersburg between operations, one of the boys in my homeroom asked me to the Friday night dance. I was still wearing bandages, so felt a little hesitant to go, but he encouraged me. It so happened that the photographer from the local newspaper was there. He took our photo and it was on the main section of the local news the next day.

I stopped counting at twenty-two operations. Each time I arrived in Michigan, the whole neighborhood came out to welcome me. Every time I went to the hospital, they all came out and waved to me. I was so blessed to have wonderful parents, aunts, uncles, cousins, and neighborhood support. They encouraged and uplifted me during all those operations that started in the 8th grade and went through my second year of college. I was always thankful to the Lord for His keeping me safe. Although my parents weren't with me, I was never afraid. I always said I was not an athlete, but I was a good sport. And best of all, God was beside me all the way.

Sixteenth Birthday Party

I'll never forget my sixteenth birthday party. It was special. It was four months after I accepted Jesus as my Savior at the Christian & Missionary Alliance Church in St. Petersburg, Florida. It was a total surprise. I'm not sure how anyone in the church knew it was my birthday because I didn't know the congregation very well. But I was there every time the door was open once I became a Christian. I played my saxophone in the orchestra at every service seven days a week. During the tourist season, there was one evangelistic meeting after another in all the churches in town. Famous evangelists and pastors from all over the world visited the city of St. Petersburg.

A month before my birthday the pastor announced a beach picnic was to be held at the St. Petersburg beach. He said it was time to have a break from the busy daily services and enjoy a family gathering at the beach. The beach is between the Gulf of Mexico and Tampa Bay. It's a barrier community located just off the Pinellas County mainland. The beach in that location and the Gulf waters are unspoiled. He warned about the sea turtle hatching tracks we all needed to watch out for as we collected shells. I was excited and my Sunday school class and youth group were going to put on a play. The fellas were in charge of the bonfires, and the mothers were in charge of the food. One member owned a grocery store, and he would provide a huge cake with chocolate ice cream in his portable cooler. We could even go swimming, as two of the members were lifeguards.

I didn't think the date would ever come, but it did. My folks sent enough fried chicken for everyone. I thought that was unusual, but I was happy. When I arrived with the family that always picked me up for church, I was shocked to see practically the whole congregation, a huge group of people. They had chairs, blankets, and the bonfire already blazing. I was in awe. We went swimming, looked for sea turtles, and collected shells. A place was set up for us to get out of our wet bathing suits, and all the young people sat on blankets.

We had hot dogs, fried chicken, potato chips, baked beans, potato salad, and homemade root beer to drink. I was in hog heaven! The pastor, who had red hair like me, led us in prayer and asked what songs or choruses we wanted to sing. We sang several songs and one man played his baritone. I wondered why he hadn't told me to bring my saxophone. Then someone requested everyone sing "Happy Birthday" and I wondered whose birthday it was. They all turned to me and sang "Happy Birthday"! They brought out a huge cake with my name on it! I was overwhelmed with joy! My parents had known about this, but they kept it a surprise for me. They weren't able to attend because of Dad's work. I have been loved all my life. I'm so thankful for everyone who helped me grow in the Lord through the years.

Bible on My Nightstand

When flying back and forth for my operations, I had a lot of time to think. About half way through them, I wasn't reading much as I had a few annoying headaches. During this time, I wore a lot of bandages on my head and had skin removed from my legs to use on my forehead. I had excellent care at the University of Michigan hospital in Ann Arbor. The nuns, aunts and uncles, cousins, and neighbors came to see me every day. When my uncle got off work, he and my aunt drove up to see me at the hospital, seven days a week. They never missed a day. My aunt wrote my mother three times a week to keep her up to date on how I was feeling. I was most fortunate, as I always healed quickly, but it took time to feel comfortable walking. That's when I realized how serious the operations actually were.

When I arrived back home by plane, I was always excited to meet my parents at the airport. When I went down the steps of the plane, I walked into tall grass. My dad took Mom and I home and he went back to work. The neighbors always came over to visit me. They brought cookies or jam they said they had made especially for me.

A family of five used to drop in for a visit and invite me to Sunday school. They never missed a Sunday picking me up, and I enjoyed them very much. The Sunday school teacher was a Swedish lady. She asked me to drop by her house on the way home from school, and she would give me a snack and read to me from the Bible. She kept her Bible on the nightstand by her bed. She had one daughter my age who was in my class. The daughter asked me to go with her on Sunday nights. She encouraged me to play my saxophone with two other people who played a baritone and a flute. It was a strange combination, but everyone liked it, and I did too. They taught me more about how to transpose music. Hymns became more real to me. After the evening service, we all went out for an ice cream cone. Sometimes we even got double dips with chocolate on top. This was a lot of fun.

The Sunday night that I accepted Jesus as my personal Savior, I knelt, I prayed, I stood up and turned around. Everyone was crying because they were so happy. I felt and knew I was a different person. When I got home, I asked my dad if I could use his Bible. He went and got it, and my mom brought in a nightstand to put beside my bed to hold the Bible.

The next time I went to have my next operations, I took my Bible that the family of five I rode with back and forth to church had given me. I not only went with them on Sunday mornings and evenings, but also on Wednesday nights to prayer meetings. When I checked into the hospital the next time I took out my Bible and placed it on the nightstand beside the bed. My doctor came in and asked me if I read it. I told him I read it every day. He said that he wished he knew more about the Bible. I told him I would tell him every day what I had read or what the nurse read to me. That is exactly what I did.

Cars

When you are young, you can hardly wait until you can drive a car. In my case, my uncle taught me to drive when I was thirteen. He had a sharp, shiny-looking brand-new green Buick. I thought it was the cat's meow. I was visiting my aunt and uncle in Dearborn, Michigan. The three of us drove to Vernors Ginger Ale store that had a soda fountain located on the banks of the Detroit River. This was a special occasion because I was their special houseguest. They made me feel very important.

The three of us were laughing and cutting up. Uncle Ed, even after working all day, was in a funny mood. Aunt Emma was always nervous when he was showing off. He was zigzagging in and out of traffic, hollering to people in the car next to him at lights, blowing smoke rings in the air, honking the horn, waving when he didn't know the people, tickling my aunt, and taking his hands off the wheel for a minute or two which seemed like hours. I was having such a good time. I thought they were the best uncle and aunt in the whole wide world.

We finally arrived at Vernors Ginger Ale store, and we three sat on bright green stools at the soda fountain bar that could swirl round and around. I had to stop swirling, as I was getting dizzy. Aunt Emma did not like to swirl the stools around, but Uncle Ed made them swirl very fast. Uncle Ed was short with red curly hair, and his feet did not even touch the ground when he sat on a stool. He had to grab onto the counter to make the stool stop.

They told me I could order anything I wanted. I thought I was in heaven with all the choices of Vernors Ginger Ale on the menu. I ordered a house soda with vanilla ice cream and a red cherry on top. When they added the ginger ale, it foamed all the way to the top and down the sides. Yum. It was so good. My uncle had a double shake with vanilla ice cream. My aunt had a banana split with three flavors of ice cream and a glass of Vernors Ginger Ale on the side. We emptied our dishes, and were stuffed by the time we left. No evidence was left of what we had been served.

As we left, Uncle Ed said it was time for me to learn to drive, so he told me to get behind the wheel. He sat on the passenger's side. My aunt sat in the back seat behind him. I was so excited, but I didn't know the first thing to do. He told me to turn the key and start the motor, which I did. Then he showed me reverse gear, and I moved the car faster than I should have. I was lucky no one was behind me, as the car moved almost a block. Next, he had me shift into first gear, and off we went with a bumpety, bump, bump, bump. He then hollered for me to shift into second, which I did, but I forgot to use the clutch. Arghhh! An awful sound, but I caught on, and used the clutch again when I shifted finally into third. By then I was keeping up with traffic.

Meanwhile, my aunt was a nervous wreck. She was trying to be polite, but it was difficult for her, because she knew I was going to hit one of the cars on the freeway. My uncle kept telling her, "Shut Up! Don't make Joan nervous! She is doing OK." I finally arrived back at their house, and flew up their driveway, swiping a little tree planted next to the sidewalk. I came to an abrupt halt three inches from the garage door.

Everyone got out. They were wiping perspiration from their faces. I was not sweaty at all. I'd had such a good time! I said, " Thank you, Uncle Ed, for teaching me to drive. I loved driving your shiny green Buick. The Vernors Ginger Ale soda was so good. When can I drive you there again?" Aunt Emma piped up, "Let's wait awhile. So much ice cream and ginger ale is not good for you. Oh, we'll go again. The radio says we are going to have rain for the next week or so."

We all went into the house happy as bugs. The opportunity didn't present itself for me to drive them again while I was there. I promised them I would be better the next time I visited them. Then I would be able to drive without help.

The next time I visited, Uncle Ed had a new, black shiny Buick. I don't know why he didn't offer to let me drive. I'd enjoyed it so much. They told the story of me driving their new, shiny green Buick to all my aunts and uncles for years. The story never died out.

I Learned It Myself

Here I am, 13 years of age, on a hot summer day driving my Uncle Ed's bright, shiny new Buick for the first time on the freeway in Detroit. Honking cars zoom past and drivers shout bad words, while I try to figure out how to shift gears, so I can go faster. Uncle Ed sits beside me, happy as a lark with the windows down, smoking his Lucky Strike, while Aunt Emma shouts from the back seat to tell me what to do before we are all killed.

Finally, I put my hand on the red-shaped ball on the gearshift and try to shift. It sounds like my dad in the Café Kitchen grinding hamburger for the noon meal. Aunt Emma screams with her hands over her eyes, and in a very shaky, shrill voice, keeps repeating that we're going to hit the truck in the lane next to us. Uncle Ed throws his cigarette butt out the window, and in a calm voice tells me to pick up my left foot and jam the left pedal down to the floor. I do what he tells me to do and keep my foot on the pedal down to the floor. A high-pitched guttural sound comes from Aunt Emma. I still don't know what to do, but decide to pull the gearshift straight down by gripping the red ball on top and I take my foot off the pedal in a hurry. The car chokes and bounces all over the freeway. The only one talking now is Aunt Emma from the back seat. Uncle Ed lights another Lucky Strike and tells me to try it again. This time I was to let the clutch out very slowly after shifting with my left foot. I move over close to the door in order to use my right foot as a spare, but that doesn't work. Uncle Ed keeps watching me, smiling as he puffs away on his cigarette. By now Aunt Emma is so hoarse she can't holler, let alone scream anymore.

I finally figure it out! First, before starting the car, I leave it in neutral, sort of in the center. Then, when ready, I jam the clutch down with my left foot and shift into first gear. Next, I jam the clutch down and go into second. Then, only one more gear to go. This is really getting to be fun!

Suddenly I see a ramp, swerve over two lanes, race to the curb, and stop with a sudden jerk. I run into the grimy neighborhood store where no one speaks English, point to the shelf of cigarettes, slap down four bits, and say, "Keep the change." I hurry out and throw the pack of cigarettes through the window. They land on Uncle Ed's lap. I race around to the other side of the car, plop myself on the seat, turn the key, and roar the engine loudly. Then I discover cars block me in, both in front and behind. We sit there awhile until the car in back finally leaves. That's good, but how in the world do I ever go backwards? Oh well, I'll just try every gear gently. First, I jam the clutch down with my left foot. Reverse isn't hard to find, as the car didn't go backwards in any of the other three gears, so I put it in neutral with the car running. I wiggle the gearshift a little here and there, and finally it dawns on me that there is some space. I jam my left foot down again, gently ease the gearshift up all the way to the top left, and gradually let the clutch out. I'm moving backwards! Going backwards makes me a little nervous. My Uncle Ed is as calm as ever! Aunt Emma is hysterical and perspiring profusely! Her beautiful starched, flowered dress is wet around the collar all the way down to her bosoms.

I let the clutch out too fast as I pull back out onto the freeway, and I drive up the ramp I just came off! Again, I can't understand why all the drivers swerve their cars this way and that way, honk their horns, and shout bad words. Some even give me the finger. Uncle Ed just keeps puffing away, one cigarette after another. Aunt Emma by this time is very quiet, leaning halfway out the window. As we approach home, Uncle Ed says, "You did well, Joanie. I knew you could figure out how to drive my car. Next time when you go in and get me a pack of cigarettes, get me Lucky Strike. This brand smells bad."

I Need My Space

Everyone I talk to says that they need their space. I am one of them too. I need my space. Life can feel frustrating when you don't have your space. When don't you have your own space that you can call your own? You don't have your own space when you're on a plane. Oh sure, the seat is reserved for you, but you're "stuffed" into it. Many times I've wished for legroom on a flight and I'm not a physically large person. It always seems that if I just had another six inches of space, I could be a lot more comfortable. Space is only a five-letter word, and yet it is so important. Astronauts and astronomers meet in space and share their views. The distance between observable objects is space. Just what is so important about having your own space?

I always wanted a bedroom of my own growing up, so I could have my so-called space. My folks never owned a house till after I graduated and had my first teaching position. By then I had moved away; that was too late. When I lived at home, it was always a one-room apartment. So naturally a small space was made for me on the screened-in porch when we lived in the South, or a space in the living room when we lived in the North. I was always comfortable, but I wanted my own space.

I was visiting my folks on my first spring break from teaching. Talking to my mother, I thought the local bank would give them a mortgage on a small house on the outskirts of town, if they had a reasonable down payment. My mother didn't think so. They didn't have a bank account. I suggested they open one. I offered to go to the bank with her. We would gather all the savings hidden in the house and deposit it.

This was an unreal experience. We ransacked every space in every room. Dollars were in the space between the mattress and the springs. Dollars were in the spaces between pictures and the backings of the frames. In the closet where clothes were hung, the rods were hollow, and dollars were jammed into those empty spaces. If there was a gap anywhere, dollars were stuffed into the space. It was unbelievable how my mother could save wherever there was room. I remember my dad asking for money to buy some socks, and Mother told him he'd have to wait till next week, as she couldn't go into their savings. My dad had no idea. Mother always had what she called a "secret space" to save.

We finally had looked everywhere imaginable. The money we found was all over the bed. We counted it and put it in stacks of ten dollars each. Then we rubber-banded the ten-dollar stacks and put them in stacks of one hundred. We finally totaled it up, and we had five thousand dollars. It was a shock not only to me, but also to my mother. We put the money in a grocery bag. It was a very hot afternoon. We drove in my car to the bank with the windows closed, doors locked, and used no air-conditioning. When we arrived at the bank, the coast looked clear, so we walked in with perspiration rolling down off our faces. I walked up to the teller and told her we needed some space away from everyone to count our money and then to make a deposit. I asked the teller to sit with us, show us how to make a deposit, and help us open a bank account. My mother was very nervous. She was breathing heavily. When we were ready to leave, the teller told us it would take three weeks before my mother could write a check. The reason was that the bills all had to be checked to make sure it was not stolen money. My poor mother sat down in a nearby chair to catch her breath and gather her thoughts. The teller assured her that everything would be all right. Driving home, Mother wondered how you would ever know, when you received your pay, which was always in cash in a brown envelope at that time, if your pay was actually stolen money. My mother received a letter in the mail the following week stating that everything was in order.

The next school break I went to visit my folks again, and we found a small home on the outskirts of the city. The builder of the home was very nice. I went with my folks to the bank and helped them fill out the forms for a mortgage. They were refused a loan, which was only two thousand dollars, because of my dad's age. I went in to talk to the manager of the bank. I told him that they had nothing to lose. The bank would get the house and make a profit, if my parents didn't make the payments. I don't know how it happened, but the manager okayed the loan. With every tip my dad made at work, my mother went right to the bank and made a payment. They not only made their monthly payments, but my mother walked to the bank three or four times some weeks just to pay a few dollars. Her payment was being revised all the time.

Their home was debt free two years before my dad passed away. When I visited them in their two-bedroom home, my dad always said, "How wonderful it is that we all have our own space now. I never thought we could give you a bedroom of your very own."

It's wonderful to have your own space whether it is a room, nook, garden, porch, or a chair you call your own. Your space gives you a feeling of freedom, a time to breathe, and a break away from everything. No matter where it is, your *space* is just for you.

I need my space, do you?

Dad, Me and Mom in St. Petersburg, Florida

CHAPTER 7

ETERNALLY SECURE

My First Bible Study

One of the girls in my class asked me to attend a Bible study. I'd never heard of a Bible study before and asked her what you do at a Bible study. My friend couldn't believe what I told her. She told me that Bible studies were like Sunday school classes. The only difference was that it wasn't on Sunday mornings, but after school during the week. I told her I would talk to my mother, and think about attending. I really liked going to Sunday school and listening to some of the stories from the Bible. Every story was new to me. Mother she said it was okay to go, if that was what I wanted to do. She couldn't believe that I'd give up swimming or riding my bicycle somewhere to listen to another Bible story. So the next day I told my friend I would go with her a couple of times to see if I liked it.

The Bible study teacher was Mrs. Ruth Munce. She was a friendly person, rather quiet, but her stories about her life at the first class were very interesting to me. She told about being a missionary and about writing romance stories. She got my attention right away! I loved to read. I had never met a missionary, nor a person who could write books. She said her mother wrote many Christian romance books, and after her mother went home to be with the Lord, Ruth started writing stories, just like her mother.

I went right home after the first meeting and repeated every word to my mother that Mrs. Munce had said. Mom suggested I read some of her books. School was almost out for the summer, and the family that took me to Sunday school and church every week not only had read all of her mother's books, but also all of her books. They told me that they enjoyed the books so much and that I could read theirs. The following week my friend said she had a surprise for me. I didn't have the foggiest idea what the surprise would be. When they dropped me off, they opened the trunk of the car and carried a box to the swing on the screened porch. It was all the books written by my Bible study teacher and her mother, Grace Livingstone Hill. Ruth gave them to me as a present for always being ready on time when they picked me up on Sunday mornings and for being so much fun. I was so happy! We hugged and laughed, and I told her that I'd tell her when they picked me up on Sunday about the books I'd read during the week. It ended up being more than one. I was skipping the religious parts. That made the books fast!

I read two of the books before the following Sunday, and I could hardly wait to tell them what I read. They remembered the stories, and we had a fun time talking about the romance books of Mrs. Munce and her mother. They had lived in the area where the stories took place, which made them even more interesting.

Years later when I visited a friend in Florida, we visited Mrs. Ruth Munce on her 101st birthday. When the elevator door opened on an upper floor of the building she lived in, she was sitting in a chair wearing a red-flowered skirt and a lovely, white crispy-starched blouse. When she saw me, she said, "Joanie, how nice of you to come and visit me!" What a memory! It had been about forty years since I had been a student in her Bible study!

Collecting Shells on the Beach

Mom and I loved to collect shells at the St. Petersburg Beach. We took advantage of every opportunity early in the morning to catch the trolley or city bus to go to the beach. As soon as the bus let us off, we went right to the beach cement wall, took our sandals off, walked down to our favorite spot by one of the trees, set down our two buckets, spread out our blanket, put our sundresses and towels in the cloth beach bag that mom made, and walked slowly down toward the water getting sand in-between our toes.

We walked along the beach beside each other with our buckets and picked up shells that were not broken and the ones half-buried in the sand. Sometimes we found a star-shaped shell. We walked for an hour or so, then went back to our blanket to put on sunscreen, as we were beginning to get warm. My mother had blond hair with brown eyes and tan skin; her parents were from northern Sweden. I took after my dad's side of the family whose parents came from England. My dad was a towhead with blue sparkling eyes and beautiful white skin. He always wore a straw hat and long sleeves, and he still got sunburned. Mother and I rubbed each other with sunscreen, more on me than on Mom. I had red, curly hair with white skin and some freckles. I still ended up with redness. My mom looked more beautiful than ever!

Next we left our buckets on the blanket and walked up and down the beach. We jumped into the waves here and there. It seemed like every time we turned around, the waves knocked us to our knees. We held hands and slowly walked out to the sandbar. Peaceful silence came over us there. We sat down for a short time and then held hands and slowly walked back to the beach, waves hitting us on our backs and shoulders and sometimes rolling over our heads.

Back at our blanket, we looked over our shells, kept the good ones, and put them all in one bucket. Then we set out again, walking another section of the beach, picking up shells and dropping them very carefully in the bucket. We never got tired of looking for different kinds of shells and walking till we could barely walk any more. By the time we got back to our blanket, it was time to pack up and catch the bus home. We washed the sand off our legs and feet in the outside showers and put our sandals back on.

Usually on the way home I fell asleep. My mother would gently whisper in my ear to wake me up when we got to the corner of Williams Park where we lived a block away. We knew the bus driver, and he got out of the bus and stood at the bottom step and held our buckets till we got off. At home we placed every shell out on the grass in the back yard, hosed them down with water, and left them to dry till the next day. Mother had some leftover spaghetti for us to eat and off to bed I went. I faintly heard Mother greet Dad when he came home from work. Collecting shells was always a wonderful day.

Wavy Hair, Water, Knees, Silver Light

Unbeknown to her, I looked at a lovely lady with silver, wavy hair. Every strand of her hair was in place. Each strand was shiny and glowing. It reminded me of the beach where I walked along the sand with my mother when I was a child. The full moon shone on waves of water hitting the shoreline. The waves gained momentum as they got closer and closer to the shore. Large waves took over smaller waves, and the light from the full moon made them sparkle a second or two. As the darkness slowly descended into the water, my mother and I walked out until it reached our knees, a good, tingly, cool feeling. As waves hit our knees, the light from the full moon enabled us to see farther down in the water. What a glorious tranquil feeling, being with someone you love so much and experiencing the inward feeling of God's creation encircling your very being. With toes relaxed deep in the sand, I squeezed my mother's hand. Mother gently squeezed my hand three times which meant *I love you.* In return, I squeezed her hand three times.

What makes this a wonderful experience? Why do we feel warm and safe beyond all harm from experiences like these? Is it the waves gaining momentum as they hit the shore? Is it warm water circling our legs up to our knees? Is it a full moon shining on the waves and hitting the shoreline, seeming to reach down and touch all this? Is it being with our mother all alone? I believe it is everything *He* has at the moment where we are, to demonstrate *His* love for us.

Salvation Army Band

I was always fascinated with the Salvation Army. They used to play downtown where I lived in Florida. They wore uniforms, and their brass instruments were very shiny. I played a saxophone and knew I could never be in the band, but I would sit on one of the green benches on the main street and listen to them. They took breaks and walked around telling everyone about the Lord.

This was all new to me, and I liked it. Some of the men and women were high-ranking officers, as they had joined the Salvation Army when they were young, and their parents were Salvation Army officers. They praised God and witnessed to the saving power of Jesus through performing high quality music. They played in all the parades and were outstanding musicians. They always started with *Onward Christian Soldiers*.

A family who were retired Salvation Army missionaries moved into the big house on the corner across the street from where we lived. They were returning home from China and brought their orange-colored Chinese chow dog with them. It had more hair than I had ever seen on a dog. Some of the children in the neighborhood called it a puffy lion. It had a dark purple tongue. The family was nice, but the dog didn't have anything to do with anyone except its own family.

Three students in my junior high school homeroom were Salvation Army children. They played their instruments in the school band and orchestra. They always got first chair in their section. One of the boys always carried my saxophone case as well as his instrument case. We became good friends and his parents had me over for dinner many times. I enjoyed his parents and his older sister who was in high school. She taught me how to transpose music. The three of us got together sometimes during the week and played hymns.

They invited me to their two-week summer camp. My mother said I could go, and I was given a scholarship. Going to a camp was a first for me. The camp was fun, especially the campfires at night with singing and testimonies. I had never heard a testimony before. Campers told how much Jesus meant to them. This camp was the first time I heard about having Jesus in your heart, and I saw campers go forward when the altar call was given to accept Jesus as their personal Savior. I could hardly wait for camp to be over, so I could go home and tell my dad and mom all about it. Each cabin had a counselor. She prayed for each one of us girls. This was all very new to me, as I'd only said the short prayer by memory *Now I lay me down to sleep*. She told me that for now, that was okay.

Summer was over too soon as usual, and I was back in school. The director of the Salvation Army asked me to be the first saxophone player to join them in their band when they performed at night on the street in the city. I was excited to be asked! My folks told me it was a good experience for me, and they said that the people were nice. I played all three years of junior high and also my first year of high school. What I learned about marching music, the Bible, and the Salvation Army was such a blessing to me!

Birthday Party

Birthday parties were always fun for me, not only as a child, but also as an adult. Most of them were surprises when I was a child. I knew when my birthday was, but never paid attention to what day it was going to be in my birthday month. My folks went all out. My red, white and blue cake with candles galore surrounded by streamers in every nook and cranny was the best!

Mother asked what kind of a cake I wanted for my birthday. I was seven years old. I was very patriotic, as my grandpa who came from the "old country" always had an American flag on the wall in his living room. My dad, who was a soldier in WWI, always marched in the July 4th parade with his regiment. He hung a USA flag out the window of our fourteenth-floor apartment building for every patriotic holiday. My folks, grandparents, all my aunts, uncles, and cousins by the dozens were proud to be citizens of the best country in the world, America. I thought for what seemed like a long time to my mother, and finally said, "I would like a red, white and blue cake that goes all the way up to the chandelier hanging from the ceiling!" My mother sort of gasped, "Oh my!"

Every apartment in the building was just alike, no matter what floor. Every kitchen had an icebox and a covered milk box next to the door in the hallway. Murphy pull-down beds were in the two bedrooms. A glass chandelier hung from the ceiling in the middle of the dining room. The one bathroom was barely big enough to turn around in. It had a toilet, a small sink jammed next to it on one side, and a tub on the other side. When you stepped out of the tub, you had to walk sideways to get out the door.

The day before my birthday, I was standing outside the school waiting for my friends. I knew I was a little late walking home because I'd had to deliver a set of crayons to the special talented art class students. It was way on the other side of the building on the second floor. I liked to be sent on these important errands. It was interesting to see all the other classrooms and the kids staying after school for music lessons, art, band, choir, detention for being late or not turning in homework, or last, but not least, smoking in the girls' or boys' lavatories.

I thought, "Where in the world are my friends? Oh, I'll start walking home. They'll show up." But not a one did. I walked up the steps into the apartment building, rang the buzzer so I could get in, checked the many mailboxes to see if we had a letter from my grandma or favorite aunt, and peeped in the door of my favorite neighbor from Greece. She always gave me a sweet to eat, but this time she said they were still in the oven. I didn't think much about it and ran up the flights of stairs to the seventh floor. I stopped just inside the doorway of Mrs. Filice from Italy. She always gave me a slice of home made bread, so I could dip it in one of her sauces, but she did not do it this time. She said the sauce was not quite done. This was a first, and I thought it was rather strange. So off I went, jumping two stairs at a time to finally get to the fourteenth floor where I lived, and the door was closed. This was really strange. The doors in the apartment building were never closed. They were always open.

Just as I opened the door, and called out, "Mom!" all my friends that lived in the apartment house shouted, "Happy Birthday, Joanie!" Whew, what a surprise! "OK," my friend, Anna, said. "Let's get to the table and eat. I'm starved." We all rushed through the dining room door to the table. What a sight to behold! A red, white and blue cake with many layers reached to the chandelier. It had an American flag on the very top with candles all around it. Each plate had a small flag on it with colored red, white and blue sandwiches. Everyone gave me a gift wrapped in red, white or blue paper.

"Thank you, Mother! I love you very much! You are the most wonderful mother in the whole wide world!" I hugged and kissed her until she said she was out of breath. What a birthday party! I shall never forget it!

Favorite Birthday Party

This glorious event took place in Cleveland, Ohio, the *Buckeye State*. I was all of ten years old in the fifth grade at Hough Elementary School. Cleveland was a wonderful place to live as a child. Lake Erie is one of the five large freshwater Great Lakes in North America. It is the 13th largest natural lake in the world. I loved to nose dive into it. I tried ever so hard to reach the bottom, but never did of course because it's around sixty-two feet deep. Lake Erie is fed from the Detroit River. Many weekends my mother and I took a small steamboat down the Detroit River. The Cuyahoga River flows through Cuyahoga Falls right through the city of Cleveland. The Cleveland Lakefront State Park in the heart of Cleveland had sandy beaches where you could build sand castles, huge rocks where you could jump from one to another, tree-lined picnic areas, and a breath-taking panoramic view of the lake along the shoreline.

Even though my mother and I took turns going to Lake Erie, Cuyahoga River, the Detroit River steamboat trip, and the Cleveland Lakefront State Park every weekend, I got to choose this time where I wanted us to go since it was my 10th birthday. I chose to go to the Cleveland Lakefront State Park. My dad was unable to join us, as he was a chef. Weekends were the busiest times of the week in the restaurant. I loved building castles in the sand with motes around them to hold water. It was fun after a castle was built to change the flow of water. That eventually wore down the walls of the mote, and the castle slowly crumbled to the ground.

The Mayor of Cleveland at this time was Harold Hitz Burton. He was a very friendly person. He and his wife, Selma, often took walks down along the beach. They held hands and laughed a lot. They admired my sand castle, so I just had to tell them it was my birthday. Some other people gathered around and they all sang *Happy Birthday* to me. Then Mr. Burton reached in his pocket and gave me a dollar coin. It was a first for me to even see a dollar coin, let alone own one.

Not only did I have this grand experience on my birthday, but also my mother asked what kind of cake I wanted. I'd just met the Mayor of Cleveland and his wife, so I felt extra patriotic. I wanted a red, white and blue cake.

Mother also told me I could invite anyone to my birthday party that I wanted.

The party was going to be in our apartment building on the fourteenth floor at two o'clock in the afternoon. I invited all the children on the first, seventh and fourteenth floors. The first floor was where the Greek families lived. The Italian families lived on the seventh floor. Scandinavian families lived on the fourteenth floor. These were my favorite floors, my favorite foods, and my favorite friends. The doors to all the apartments were always open, so you could go in, play and usually have something to eat. Oh, how I enjoyed living in this apartment building!

My mother said she'd call me when she had everything ready. The time finally came, and the word spread fast. There were dozens of friends outside in the hallway waiting for my mother to open the door, and finally she did. It was a patriotic sight to behold I'll never forget as long as I live. The dining room table was in the center of the room, and the chandelier hung from the ceiling. Its lights were on, and all other lights in the other rooms were off. The cake was decorated red, white and blue with a red layer, then a white layer, and then a blue layer and then one layer after another in red, white and blue till it reached the chandelier. We were all excited! All my friends hooted and hollered and wished me a Happy Birthday. Some of my friends' mothers came in to help my mother cut and serve the cake and ice cream to the dozens of children from the first, seventh, and fourteenth floors. Everyone sat on the floor. When we had all been served, including the ones who had second helpings, they sang "Happy Birthday, dear Joanie! Happy Birthday to you!"

We were allowed to eat all the cake and ice cream we wanted. Then we clamored out the door and raced down the fourteen flights of stairs to the street to play Kick the Can till we were exhausted. When our mothers called us to come in, we were happy to do so. By this time the sun was going down. It was a custom at the end of the day before we all went to our own floors, to climb the stairs to the roof for half an hour or so. Up there at the top, we listened to the sounds of the city, watched the boats on the lakes and the birds fly in to find their resting places at the end of the day. What a wonderful birthday to remember when I lived in Cleveland, Ohio at the age of ten with my friends on the first, seventh, and fourteenth floors!

When Is Your Birthday?

SINCE JESUS CAME INTO MY HEART
Rufus H. McDaniel 1914

What a wonderful change in my life has been wrought
since Jesus came into my heart!
I have light in my soul for which long I had sought
since Jesus came into my heart!

I have ceased from my wandering and going astray
since Jesus came into my heart!
And my sins, which were many, are all washed away
since Jesus came into my heart!

I'm possessed of a hope that is steadfast and sure
since Jesus came into my heart!
And no dark clouds of doubt now my pathway obscure
since Jesus came into my heart!

There's a light in the valley of death now for me
since Jesus came into my heart!
And the gates of the city beyond I can see
since Jesus came into my heart!

I shall go there to dwell in that City I know
since Jesus came into my heart!
And I'm happy so happy as onward I go
since Jesus came into my heart!

Since Jesus came into my heart,
Since Jesus came into my heart
Floods of joy o'er my soul like the sea billows roll
since Jesus came into my heart!

Birthdays have always been special in my family. My folks always remembered my birthday, and they went "all out". It was a fun time. I always had a special cake with all the letters, peeled from a shiny paper bought in McCrory's Dime Store. The candles matched the letters. They prepared my favorite food. They invited my school and neighborhood friends. When we lived by my cousins, they were invited too. The birthday party was in the afternoon after school or on a Saturday morning until junior high school. Then the birthday party took place on a Friday night usually with the folks in the kitchen and all my friends in the front room playing games like Kick the Can, Spin the Bottle and Treasure Hunt. In high school we wanted to do something grown up, so we met in the drugstore for hours eating hot dogs and French fries and drinking root beer sodas until we almost gagged. Even though my parents didn't have much money, they made sure I always had a present on special days. My favorite birthday present was a watch in my first year of junior high school. It was hard to concentrate on studies as I looked at that watch all day in class. I had a special handkerchief on my dresser where I carefully placed my watch every night when I went to bed, so it wouldn't get scratched.

In fifth grade I got a brown and white bicycle for Christmas. I rode that bicycle everywhere. I really thought I was something. My bicycle finally rusted out by eighth grade, so my uncle taught me to drive in his new Buick on the freeway. I'd graduated from two wheels to four wheels! My mother loved for me to drive her to the stores every day. I was the only one in my class who had a car to drive. I had to take my dad to and from work every day, so that I could have the car for the day.

I drove my folks' car to Sunday school and church. Friends went with me who never went to Sunday school and church just so they could ride with me in the car! Those were fun days. But things changed. I became a sophomore in high school. Then I not only went to church on Sunday mornings, but I also started going to evening services. I played saxophone in a combo for the services. I enjoyed everything but the preaching. I stayed to listen to the preacher, as the combo played during the altar call and for ten minutes after the service. The Sunday evening of January 11, 1948 my dad had to cook at a special barbecue on the beach for the soldiers at the VA hospital, so I didn't have the car. I was working at the Traymore Cafeteria, and I declined an offer from one of the church families to pick me up to go to the service, as I knew we wouldn't be in time for the beginning of the service. I left work and was walking through Williams Park to catch a bus home. The first bus that pulled up was not my bus to get home. This bus was going within a block of the church. On an impulse, I took it and decided I'd go to the service, as there was a special speaker. I arrived late and sat next to my Sunday school teacher. They had some special music by the male church quartet I always enjoyed, especially the deep bass singer.

Then it was time to introduce the wife of a well-known evangelist. I couldn't see her from where I was sitting. A matronly lady stood up and walked toward the pulpit. Her attire shocked me. Women in the church were very plain in those days. That is, they wore no makeup whatsoever. This lady wore a chiffon, silky-black, ornate dress with white pearls, black hose with decorations up the back of her legs, a black wide-brimmed hat with black tassels dangling down all around the rim, thick powder and bright rouge on her face, and bright, shiny lipstick above the natural line of her lips. Whew! I didn't know what to think! She got my attention! I whispered to my Sunday school teacher that this was different. She patted my hand and smiled. The redheaded, conservative young pastor stood beside her and introduced her as Mrs. Billy Sunday. He said the message tonight was "just for you" and he looked directly at me, I thought. I was a little uncomfortable. I looked at my watch and figured I would be out of there within 25 to 30 minutes. Mrs. Billy Sunday told about her husband's ministry and how God was leading her to present the same message as her husband. She presented the plan of salvation. I'm sure it had been preached many times previously, but this time it made sense to me. She made it very clear that the way you are now, you are cut off from God, and there is nothing you can do. Then she said that God loves you with unconditional love. She said several times that the only way to God is through Jesus Christ. She gave an altar call to receive Christ as your personal Savior. I felt she was looking straight at me the whole time. The people began singing the song *Pass me not, O gentle Savior. Hear my humble prayer. While on others Thou art calling, do not pass me by.* There were four verses to the song. They kept singing all four verses over and over again. I didn't think they would ever stop. This went on for about fifteen minutes that seemed like an hour as she kept saying that someone out there needs to come forward, and we are not going to close till they do. Well, finally I caught on and realized that I was a sinner, and I did not want to be one. I left my seat and walked up and knelt at the altar. My Sunday school teacher kneeled on one side of me, and the pastor's wife kneeled on the other side. It was right at that moment that I gave my heart to Jesus. The lights went on, and they have never gone out. When I stood up, I was different. I even thought different. I knew that Jesus had come into my heart.

This is the birthday I celebrate every year. January 14th is My Birthday. How many birthdays have you? Can you sing the song: *Happy Birthday to you. Happy Birthday to you. Born again means salvation. How many birthdays have you?*

Think about celebrating your birthday every year on the day you accepted Jesus as your personal Savior. I told you when it was my birthday. When is your birthday? Tell me. Let's have a real birthday party and invite our friends, neighbors, aunts and uncles, and cousins by the dozens! *Floods of joy o'er my soul like the sea billows roll, since Jesus came into my heart!*

The Splash of the Water

"Mom, my Sunday school teacher talked to me today and she thought I should be baptized since I've become a Christian, am growing in the Lord, and know what I'm doing. She also told me it's like being obedient to the Lord and is a witness to my friends that I am sincere. I told her I was baptized as a baby. I remember how you told me all about how when the minister sprinkled water on my head, I belted out a scream, started crying, and rubbed my eyes and tried to wipe the water off my head."

"Joanie, you should take the class with your friends in your Sunday school class, and learn what it's all about. I'm sure you will ask lots of questions and he'll explain what this will mean in your life. I don't know too much about it, as dad and I had to leave home before we were in our teens to find work in the city. We were only sprinkled when we were babies so we don't remember it. The certificates of our baptism are hanging in the hall of our parents' home. I've looked at them many times."

"Mom, the way they baptize you in this church is that they push you down in the water in a big pool they have inside the church in winter time, and in the summer everyone goes down to the lake to be baptized. I think my teacher said the word was immersion. I asked what it meant and she said that it was another way to say *dunking* or *dipping*."

"Why don't you just go to the class with your friends, and ask all the questions that come to your mind, and then we'll talk about it. Take this very seriously, Joanie. It's a precious event in your life."

"But mom, what if I choke when I go under the water and come up gagging and spitting?"

"Joanie, don't worry about that now. Let's take one step at a time. First, take the classes, and then you can decide if it's right for you at this time."

"Ok. I'll do it, but I want you and Dad to be there, as all the parents of my friends will be there, and it will be on the radio, as it's in the afternoon and our pastor is going to announce everyone's name over the air."

"We'll cross that bridge when we come to it."

I took all the classes. I knew it was the right time for me. My parents couldn't attend, as my dad worked on Sunday, the busiest day of the week. One of the helpers at Dad's work brought in a radio and placed it on a kitchen shelf. They turned it on, and when they said my name, everyone hooped and hollered. My mom took her little radio and held it up close to her ear in the bedroom and cried when she heard my name. She'd even heard the splash of the water. That night when Dad came home, the three of us had a special celebration. Dad had brought home a large bottle of root beer for us to share.

How Did It Happen?

It was wonderful having parents who no matter what the situation, right was right, and wrong was wrong. Many times growing up I asked my dad what he thought about this or that, and I wanted him to side in with my thinking. He gave me good advice. He always said, "Even though you don't come out on top," and "You know, Joanie," and "The good Lord knows that you should always do what is right to the best of your ability." Then I'd go to my mother to see if I could persuade her to my side in thinking out the situation and deciding what action I should take. It never worked. They thought alike. She'd say, "Joanie, what is right is right, and what is wrong is wrong. Do your best to do what is right." This annoyed me sometimes, as I wanted to do what was right, but I also wanted to make the incident favorable in my thinking. My parents were not Christians until their later years, but they had high morals and lived, as they would say, by "the golden rule".

I was the first in our family to become a Christian. They respected my decision, and the very next day when we came to the table for a meal, I was asked to "say the blessing" and from that very day I said the blessing at every meal. Sometimes they called the blessing a "prayer" and sometimes it was "give thanks" for the meal.

I was never taught to pray out loud, so when I prayed at the table, I prayed for my folks, aunts, uncles, cousins, friends and everything and everyone who came to my mind to accept the Lord as their personal Savior. I think I took quite a long time as my dad always said that he was glad I remembered to thank the Lord for our dinner and the hands of Mother who prepared it.

I was five years old when I first heard someone pray out loud at a meal. My folks told me just before we arrived at my aunt's house that no one starts to eat their food until everyone is served because they always said a prayer. Then we could eat. I'd never heard of such a thing, but I was anxious to hear a prayer. All I ever heard in our home was when I went to bed my mother tucked me in and knelt beside my bed. I said, "Now I lay me down to sleep. I pray the Lord my soul to keep. If I should die before I wake, I pray the Lord my soul to take." I was so impressed to hear my dad's sister, Sarah Ellen, pray. She lived in the middle of an orange grove in Plant City, Florida. She had twelve children, so you can imagine how I loved to visit them. She not only prayed for the food, but she said how happy she was to have her brother, Bob, and his family here with them. She even mentioned my name in the prayer before she said "Amen." Then everyone said "Amen."

I finished high school through correspondence after completing 11th grade in order to go to college with my friends in the fall. They were one year older than me. A group of us went to a small four-year Bible college in St. Petersburg, Florida known as *The Sunshine City*. If the sun didn't make an appearance, the St. Petersburg Times gave out a free newspaper that day. I think that twice in the thirty-five years my folks lived in St. Petersburg the sun didn't shine.

Classes always started in the chapel at the college. Prayer requests were written down daily in a large, spiral black notebook. There were three columns. I entered my parents' names in column one. Then in column two beside their names, I wrote "personal salvation." Column three was for the date of answered prayer requests. I really felt that my prayer and the prayers of their parents, brothers, sisters and friends would be answered, that they would accept Him as their personal Savior. It didn't happen while I was in Bible college, but it did happen. This is how they came to accept Jesus Christ as their personal Savior.

My dad was sitting on the front porch looking at the daily newspaper. My mother walked out, and as she looked down the street she noticed an older well-dressed man in a suit walking toward our house. She recognized the man. He was my dad's younger brother, Lloyd. She said to my dad, "Look up! That's your brother, Lloyd, walking toward our house. We've not seen him in 25 years!" My dad didn't look up, but assured her that his brother lived in Cleveland and that it was just someone who looked like him. "No, it's your brother Lloyd, and he is a changed man. I can tell that he is a different person now." Lloyd then walked right up to the porch and said, " Hi Bob." He hugged my mother. They were both stunned as Lloyd was always a heavy-drinking man, and because of his drinking he would get into a lot of trouble. This was the first time they saw him sober. Now my dad put his paper down, and they began talking and laughing. During this time, my mother made coffee and served it with cookies, then went back into the house to prepare lunch. My dad asked Lloyd, " What are you doing here?" Lloyd put his cup down, and their crystal-clear blue eyes met. Lloyd said, "Bob, I have come to tell you how my life has been changed since I became a Christian three years ago. I want you to accept Christ as your personal Savior too. The Lord led me here to visit with you. I have visited every home now of all our six sisters and eight brothers, and I have led them to the Lord. You are the last one." My dad was known to be tough, but he really wasn't at all. He had a very soft heart. Tears came to his eyes. They bowed their heads, and Lloyd led Dad in the prayer of salvation. My mother then called them to the table. Uncle Lloyd said the blessing, thanking Him for such a good lunch prepared by my mother. He prayed for my dad to grow in the Lord and for my Mother to accept Jesus as her Savior. He did not convince her. He thanked her for the lovely lunch. He had to leave to catch the bus back to where he was staying with his sister, Sarah Ellen, in Plant City, Florida.

My dad got up from the table and fainted. My mother called the doctor, and he came right away. My dad said that he was going to take a nap. My mother then called me and told me that my Dad fainted and was taking a nap. She would like me to fly home, as she thought it was serious. I questioned her, but she said in all their years of marriage he had never fainted, and he never took a nap. I caught the next flight home. I sat on the bed beside my dad, and we talked about his brother and how he had led him to the Lord. He told me to pray for Mother, as she really didn't understand. I was holding my dad's hand when he told me that he loved Mother and I. His eyes closed and he peacefully went home to be with the Lord.

Several years later, I was living with my husband and two sons in Central Africa. I wrote every day to my mother. During our nine years in Africa, I was able to visit my mother three times. She was a different person. It was the first time in my life that my mother didn't stay home and prepare dinner when I went to church on Sunday morning. She got dressed and went with me. I was elated to introduce my mother to all my friends, and they were happy to meet her. My mother told me that she went with one of my girlfriends from college to a Bible study at her church once a week. This was a surprise to me!

All those years, my mother's excuse for not attending church had been due to her hearing problem. She listened to the radio every night in bed and put the radio up to her ear to listen to her favorite programs. One night a preacher explained the plan of salvation. He asked the listeners to repeat a prayer after him; she accepted the Lord as her Savior. Mom wrote the date in her Bible that I'd given her when I was in Bible college. My girlfriend wrote me that there was not a doubt in her mind that my mother was now a Christian. I was overwhelmed with joy, and thankful for how the Lord works in our lives and in the lives of our loved ones.

I remembered how I wrote in column one and two in that large three-column, black spiral notebook. All the students pray daily for every entry during chapel. It was a blessing three decades later when I visited the college that now there was an entry in column three for my mother. How did it happen? It happened in His right timing and through faithful prayers of students, friends and family.

The hymn speaks to all of us.

FOR YOU I AM PRAYING

Ira Sankey 1864

I have a Savior, He's pleading in glory,
A dear, loving Savior though earth friends be few;
And now He is watching in tenderness o'er me;
And oh, that my Savior were your Savior, too.
For you I am praying,
For you I am praying,
For you I am praying,
I'm praying for you.
I have a Father; to me He has given
A hope for eternity, blessèd and true;
And soon He will call me to meet Him in Heaven,
But oh, that He'd let me bring you with me, too!
I have a robe; 'tis resplendent in whiteness,
Awaiting in glory my wondering view;
Oh, when I receive it all shining in brightness,
Dear friend, could I see you receiving one, too!
When Jesus has found you, tell others the story,
That my loving Savior is your Savior, too;
Then pray that your Savior may bring them to glory,
And prayer will be answered—'twas answered for you!

Speak of that Savior, that Father in Heaven,
That harp, crown, and robe which are waiting for you—
That peace you possess, and that rest to be given,
Still praying that Jesus may save them with you.

Teardrop

What is special about a teardrop when you see it? A teardrop has often marked very emotional times for me. I remember when I had to go to the hospital the very first time. My parents took me for a routine operation, the doctor had told my parents. I had to have my tonsils taken out. At that time they automatically removed your adenoids as well. I saw a teardrop on my mother's cheek when they rolled me into the operating room. When they returned me to my room after the operation, I was given a bowl of ice cream. Oh, it looked so good, but I couldn't swallow it. Three days later I could manage to eat the ice cream.

Every time my dad got a job far away, we had to pack up and move. Mother had teardrops on her face spilling down to her chin as we said "good-bye" to our relatives and friends. I was always okay until I saw a few teardrops bounce out of my mother's eyes. It was then that they bounced out of mine too! Some things are hard to control, and teardrops on my mother's cheeks were one of them. It seemed like they were contagious because every time Mother's cheeks got wet with teardrops, mine were soon wet too.

I never knew anyone who collected tears and saved them in a bottle. I could fill a five gallon jug with all the teardrops I've seen on faces of mothers when they saw their daughters walk down the aisles to get married; had their children baptized; attended memorial services; held newborn babies; waved goodbye to sons and daughters going off to war; watched their children receive diplomas, win special awards, score points in athletic events, receive communion, sing a song, make a profession of faith or join a church.

Teardrops spurt out of children's eyes when they don't get their own way, or when they feel bad because someone hurt their feelings. Even if they aren't hurt, children will sometimes cry when they trip or stumble.

Soon after coming home to the USA after nine years in Central Africa, we went to see a newly released film on Africa. It was a true story. The film was very real to us. We left the theatre without saying a word. We both shed a stream of flowing teardrops from our cheeks on down to the ground.

My dad was known for his strength, as well as his short fuse. He didn't mince words with his fellow workers. He worked hard and expected his staff to do the same. He was fair, honest, and very reliable. My mother and I could always count on him. He only showed emotion when it pertained to the family, except when our Toy Manchester of seventeen years fell asleep and never woke up. Dad gently picked him up, blinking away teardrops that were falling fast. It was a precious scene I shall never forget.

The last teardrop I saw was on the slim, tanned-by-the-sun finger on the left hand of my lovely girlfriend. It was a beautiful diamond-shaped, teardrop engagement ring.

What is it about a teardrop? You tell me.

What If?

The way life seems to go, it's sometimes easy to think back to *what if?*

What if I had done this or that?

What if I had finished high school with my class?

What if I had fallen when I accepted a dare and was hanging out the window of a second grade classroom?

What if I had not played softball the day I was knocked down when Susie hit the ball, and it bounced off my forehead? Whambo, down I went.

What if I had not gone out on the rowboat with a couple of friends when the oar hit me on the side of the head as Frankie turned around?

What if I had not gone skiing with my roommates, passed out several times and had to be carried down on the gurney by the ski patrol?

What if one of the ski patrols had not noticed my boots were laced too tight, cutting off my circulation?

What if the highway patrol had not noticed me passed out in the ditch beside the orange grove with my snowsuit on?

What if the streetcar had not stopped in time at the corner where I fainted on the tracks?

What if I had seen the curly-haired little black doggie run out in the street in front of my car?

What if I had not gone swimming with my friends at the public swimming pool, been shoved and hit the side of the pool?

What if our family doctor had not referred me to the plastic surgeon at the University of Michigan?

What if the plastic surgeon took one look and said there was nothing he could do for me?

What if my biological mother had not signed the adoption papers?

What if my adopted parents did not like me?

What if my dad and mother refused to help me in college?

What if I never played the saxophone in the school band?

What if I never sang in a trio?

What if my aunt didn't notice I was on the wrong turf and didn't rescue me?

What if my folks were from small families?

What if I never went to college?

What if the graduate program had not accepted my transcripts?

What if I had lived in one place all my life?

What if I was blond instead of redheaded?

What if I was born with a furry birthmark on my face?

What if I'd frozen when the elephant turned around and charged toward me?

What if I jumped out of the van before I saw the three lions sitting there?

What if I tried to retrieve the golf ball when the crocodile surfaced?

What if I jumped in the pool of water and landed on top of the hippo?

What if I caught the #4 train that caught on fire in the subway?

What if I missed the last train to Long Island at Penn Station?

What if?

What if?

What if?

And on and on it goes.

Is this the best way to think? I prefer to remember: *In all your ways acknowledge Him, and He shall direct your path. Proverbs 3: 6*

Victory in Jesus

I woke up this morning singing this hymn written by Eugene Monroe Bartlett Sr. in 1939. I haven't heard it sung in years. When I first joined the youth choir at the church I attended, that hymn was chosen by one of the choir members in our weekly Sunday night services, our mid-week prayer meetings and in our Saturday night get-togethers. After the first verse, the leader gave his testimony. Then he chose someone else to give his or her testimony after the next verse, and so on till everyone had spoken. Sometimes he had us look up scriptures to read between the verses. He always quoted John 16:33, "I have told you these things, so that in me you may have peace. In this world you will have trouble, but take heart! I have overcome the world."

The words from this well-known and treasured hymn remind each one of us that we can experience victory in Jesus every day of our lives. Yes, there is victory in Jesus! What do you think? Will you sing in heaven with me this song of victory?

VICTORY IN JESUS

E.M. Bartlett   1939

I heard an old, old story,
How a Savior came from glory,
How He gave His life on Calvary
To save a wretch like me;
I heard about His groaning,
Of His precious blood's atoning,
Then I repented of my sins;
And won the victory.

O victory in Jesus,
My Savior, forever.
He sought me and bought me
With His redeeming blood;

He loved me ere I knew Him,
And all my love is due Him,
He plunged me to victory,
Beneath the cleansing flood.

I heard about His healing,
Of His cleansing power revealing.
How He made the lame to walk again
And caused the blind to see;
And then I cried, "Dear Jesus,
Come and heal my broken spirit,"
And somehow Jesus came and brought
To me the victory.

O victory in Jesus,
My Savior, forever.
He sought me and bought me
With His redeeming blood;
He loved me ere I knew Him,
And all my love is due Him,
He plunged me to victory,
Beneath the cleansing flood.

I heard about a mansion
He has built for me in glory.
And I heard about the streets of gold
Beyond the crystal sea;
About the angels singing,
And the old redemption story,
And some sweet day I'll sing up there
The song of victory.

O victory in Jesus,
My Savior, forever.
He sought me and bought me
With His redeeming blood;
He loved me ere I knew Him,
And all my love is due Him,
He plunged me to victory,
Beneath the cleansing flood.

About the Author

Joan Hust was born in a shack without running water and electricity in Cleveland, Ohio to a single mom. Her biological mom became her aunt after adoption by her maternal uncle.

Joan's parents never finished school, and by the time Joan was in fifth grade, she had attended 25 grammar schools, yet reading was always an important part of her growing up years.

The first time she heard a prayer was when she visited another aunt's home. She heard her name used in the prayer. Joan became a Christian as a high school sophomore after hearing Mrs. Billy Sunday preach. She dropped out of school her junior year and enrolled in a 4-year Bible college in Florida graduating magna cum laude, then earned a BA at Florida Southern College and an Alumni Achievement Award. She taught all grades through junior college in Michigan, Florida, and Washington. She earned Master's Degrees at Wayne State University and Seattle University, and received an Honorary Doctorate of Literature from Florida.

Joan and her husband served as missionaries in Africa. Bill, a mechanical engineer at a copper mine, also supported her endeavors. Joan produced a children's weekly program on Zambia TV and radio, taught at the mine, parochial schools and at Theological College of Central Africa. She wrote a safari manual, led safaris in Kafue National Park and ran a printing operation in her home that supplied stationery, Bible tracts and brochures for the country. Joan was the youth leader at the local church in Chingola, Zambia. After returning from Africa, she earned a Master in Library Science at Long Island University and worked as a medical librarian in New York and Idaho.

Joan stays involved in missions by traveling to Togo, Burundi, Ethiopia, England, Scotland, Africa, Cuba, China, Guatemala and India. She helps build libraries, gives health lectures and teaches medical government databases to missionaries, pastors, government officials and local people who have access to computers. At home she speaks about missions at local churches, civic groups and schools. Joan received the Woman of Distinction Education Award 2000 sponsored by Lewis-Clark State College, North Idaho College, University of Idaho, and U of ID Research Park. Soroptimist Women's Forum awarded Joan The Woman of the Year 2008.

Joan and her husband live in Coeur d'Alene, Idaho and have three grown children and three grandchildren who live in Idaho, Washington, and Alaska.

JoanHust@live.com